SUCCESS WITH TROUT

Success on the final dibble

MC with an immaculately marked Loch Leven brownie

SUCCESS WITH
TROUT

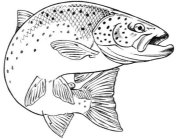

Martin Cairncross, John Dawson
and Chris Ogborne

DAVID & CHARLES
Newton Abbot   London

This book is dedicated to George,
a residential brown trout of the Itchen,
who seemed to understand more about us
than we did about him.

Trying for George

British Library Cataloguing in Publication Data
Cairncross, Martin
  Success with trout.
  I. Title II. Dawson, John III. Ogborne, Chris
  799.1'755

  ISBN 0-7153-9369-3

© Martin Cairncross, John Dawson and Chris Ogborne, 1990

Typeset in $10\frac{1}{2}/12\frac{1}{2}$pt Sabon by ABM Typographics Ltd Hull
and printed in Great Britain
by Butler & Tanner Limited, Frome and London
for David & Charles Publishers plc
Brunel House Newton Abbot Devon

CONTENTS

AUTHORS' NOTE

Whatever the angler's reason for going fishing, few would deny that 'catching fish' is the normal definition of success. There are, of course, many other motives. Anglers go fishing to enjoy the scenery, the wildlife and the surroundings, and for the therapy, as there is no finer way of reducing the tensions and pressures of everyday life than spending relaxing hours on or by the water. There are indeed times when simply being there is enough, soaking up the atmosphere of the place without actually fishing at all.

Most of the time, however, the principal enjoyment comes in actually catching fish. The joint authors of this book have collectively spent over sixty years of their lives trout fishing, during which time they have concentrated on refining their styles to achieve maximum success. Their main pre-occupation is not in achieving 'limit bags', but rather in the greater satisfaction derived from the challenge of translating their ideas into new and successful methods for tempting trout. They are totally dedicated to the sport of fly fishing, and have been individually responsible for pioneering many new techniques and fly patterns. They have also discovered some fundamental new ways of understanding trout behaviour.

This book is the outcome of the authors' research and experience and represents a labour of love. They are sharing their ideas and philosophies which hopefully are described in an acceptable and easily understandable way, and in a logical sequence which will be invaluable to both the raw novice and the seasoned expert with a full generation of fly fishing behind him.

We would like to thank Anglian Water, Bristol Waterworks Company and Southern Water for supplying us with maps and information, and extend our gratitude to all other water authorities who offer high quality fly fishing.

We also offer our sincere appreciation to the following individuals: Roger Thom for information supplied on Rutland Water; Howard MacKenzie for information supplied on Bewl Water; Chris Klee, Ian Williamson and Bob Handford for their part in providing such excellent trout fishing on our local Bristol reservoirs; Paul Knight for the many wonderful days we have enjoyed at the Langford Fishery; Jeremy Lucus, Brian Leadbetter and Dave Shipman for local advice given on fishing the major reservoirs; Richard Chidley for line diagrams and Andrew Clare for macro photography.

INTRODUCTION

EVOLUTION OF IDEAS

This book embodies original ideas which will help the thinking fly fisherman to be more successful — it is most definitely not a reconstruction of other people's writings, but relies solely on our own experiences. The three of us have not only been fishing together for many years, we have probably also spent an equal amount of time talking to each other about the trout and the methods of catching him. Sharing ideas with others is an extremely effective way of improving tactics and gives a very wide perspective on the whole subject.

Initially we had very different ideas on the best ways to catch trout. Our tactics varied from being too fanciful to downright boring, from being obsessed with the floating line to chopping and changing too often, and from being purely imitative to trying to distract the trout by any means possible. But gradually, the frequent light-hearted criticisms — 'lure stripper', 'boring' and 'purist' — began to make an impression, and minor changes and compromises in tactics started to emerge until it suddenly dawned on us that we were all using virtually the same flies and some very similar methods. This is not to say that each of us put the same emphasis on each method, but rather that we all possessed the same armoury of techniques. It had reached the stage where we had discussed them in such detail that in competitions we could call out some simple word and this would convey the precise message of how we were catching, although it was unintelligible to anyone else. We were often accused of using code, although the words had not been deliberately formulated for that purpose.

It was this realisation that our ideas had converged so closely from our detailed discussions which gave us the idea for this book. A book which gives the thoughts of a single fisherman is bound to be subjective, and if we had each put our ideas down a few years ago as individuals, the methods described would not have been nearly so effective, nor could they have undergone anything like the same degree of scrutiny which has arisen from our detailed shared research. Many of our ideas, of course, have come from talking to and fishing with other people. In some cases information is freely given, whereas quite often favourite tactics are held back as if governed by the Official Secrets Act. Competitions have provided a major contribution to exchange, both international and the Benson and Hedges series, since they present the perfect opportunity to meet and fish with people from different parts of the British Isles. Under these conditions a fisherman is always

going to pull out all the stops, and it is very hard to hide anything from an observant and alert boat partner.

The methods permitted for stillwater trout fishing vary enormously from lake to lake. Some waters allow worming, spinning and trolling, whereas others restrict methods to a single fly no larger than a size 12. Anglers' views on these regulations vary as much as the rules themselves and there will always be accusations of 'purist' or 'Philistine'. The only solution to this is to follow your own beliefs, to fish your own styles, and not to condemn anyone who is observing the rules of a fishery.

We have all done our fair share of Nobbler fishing, and had a great deal of fun in the process. Such tactics are arguably an essential part of any trout fisherman's education, but with experience the challenge and satisfaction of fly fishing comes from keeping to, and developing tactics for, a set of rules which maintain an element of skill. The effectiveness of lures such as Nobblers and Wagglers can be attributed to their in-built movement, which is nothing to do with the skill of the angler in his retrieve, and which even a well-educated trout can sometimes find irresistible. No self-respecting snooker player, for example, would want to increase his breaks by using a larger pocket, and yet many anglers will persistently use some of the most crude methods available to catch more fish.

This does not mean to say that lure fishing should in any way be condemned in favour of imitative techniques. There are many occasions when the fish are simply not interested in feeding, and the only method of catching them is by appealing to their curiosity or aggression. Whether this is accomplished with a Viva or an induced take with a Green Tag Stick Fly is irrelevant, since under these circumstances the fish has been lured into taking the fly in a manner which does not imitate his normal feeding pattern. Furthermore, there are many fishermen who stand aghast at the mention of a lure, yet they can often be seen stripping small flies across the water surface to distract or raise a trout and what they are doing is often nothing but lure fishing with a more traditional pattern. Many traditionalists will also fly fish for salmon, and an imitative approach is then impossible since a salmon will very rarely feed in fresh water.

There is, nevertheless, a fundamental difference between the use of a Stick Fly and a large Viva. The large lure has a built-in mobility because of its long marabou plumes, so the way in which it is moved through the water becomes less important. Use of the small fly (or lure), however, can require a great deal of skill in the way it is retrieved.

The pros and cons of imitative versus lure fishing could be discussed for ever, and there is such a grey area of overlap between the two that some yardstick was needed; so we tend to base our tactics on fly size alone. Our thinking is largely

Recording the catch

based on international rules, since the maximum size of less than an inch ($^{15}/_{16}$in to be precise) provides a reasonable limit in restricting the degree of automatic movement — although our approach is flexible and does cover larger insects such as damsels and mayflies. With this criterion, there is no need to argue whether a particular pattern is really a lure or not. Thus, our fly boxes include Vivas and Peach Dolls as well as Stick Flies and Buzzers, even though we do much prefer fishing imitatively when conditions allow.

The choice of international rule size in our tactics also arose from enjoyment of competition fishing. It is very easy during a normal day's fishing to depart from this approach when conditions are hard, but then there would be nothing by way of experience to fall back on during a tough competition day. Restricting one's tactics to international rules, at least for boat fishing, allows skills to be developed for these competitive occasions, and leads to greater confidence altogether.

There will be those who disagree with our assertion that to use Nobblers or to trail enormous lures resembling cockerels behind a boat are unskilful forms of fishing. But even if they were right, we would certainly not have the required skills or experience to discuss these particular tactics – such methods have no place in this book.

Only those techniques in which we are well practised have been described — a very pertinent example is short lining in front of a boat with a long rod. It is a technique which we have rarely used, and is therefore only mentioned in passing since we do not pretend to possess an expertise based merely on researching other people's work. Unlike the use of Nobblers and Cockerels, however, there is no difficulty in defending this loch-style tactic as an extremely skilful and satisfying form of fly fishing.

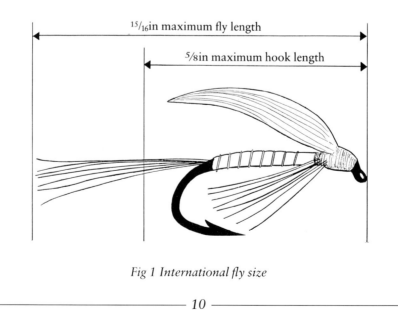

Fig 1 International fly size

In the section on tackle, no attempt is made to describe the vast array of variations available on the market today. Instead, a selection is made of only those items which are really necessary for successful results.

Before launching into tactics, the trout's behaviour and environment is discussed. Information about his food items and the ways to imitate them is easily available elsewhere, but it is unusual for much emphasis to be placed on the nature of the fish itself. This is a significant omission, because the way in which a fish will respond depends on whether he has been recently introduced or is an established resident, whether he is a brownie or a rainbow, and on the size and quality of the water.

The main part of this book discusses the methods for successful trout fishing, both from a boat and the bank. To a large extent this reiterates the information on trout behaviour since the two subjects are inextricably mixed. Obviously many of the methods are well established, but we have tried to put them into context and describe some new techniques such as FTA and forward lead.

Fly tying is dealt with in we hope a refreshingly different manner — there are many excellent books and articles whose aim is usually to explain how to tie flies which are technically correct and which will adorn any fly box. However, we prefer to show how fly-tying methods can be employed not to win prizes in fly-tying competitions, but simply to catch more fish. All the flies which comprise our own front line of attack are described, together with how and when they are used.

Our methods for boat fishing are based on international rules, and although this is not a book about competition fishing, in view of our various successes over the years — for example, the performance of Bristol Reservoirs Fly Fishers Association in the Benson and Hedges championship — we have included some tactics which are specifically aimed at competitions. Those not interested in competitions can still gain a great deal from this chapter since many of the techniques are generally suitable for pleasure fishing as well.

Throughout the book we have attempted to describe general ideas which would be applicable to a wide range of waters. Each water has its peculiarities, however, and of course there is a great deal to be learned about the contours and features which create local hot-spots. However, it would be a monumental task to try to cover all fisheries, so we have included a section devoted to just the four major waters in England: Chew, Bewl, Rutland and Grafham. And rather than attempting to deal with these reservoirs ourselves, we invited individual local experts to assist us (with the exception of Chew Valley Lake). We would therefore like to offer our warmest appreciation to Jeremy Lucas, Dave Shipman and Brian Leadbetter for responding so positively in providing us with the information required.

No fishing book would be complete without sharing a few experiences, so a few anecdotes help put our ideas into perspective — trips to the pub, the odd bottle of wine on a boat, playing the odd practical joke when the opportunity arises. This

Fishing is all about enjoyment and relaxation

aspect of fly fishing is important because like any other pastime, the emphasis should be on enjoyment. It is so easy to become pre-occupied with catching as many fish as possible at every available opportunity, that fishing becomes an obsession rather than a pleasure. Competitions add spice to the sport, but the overall purpose should be relaxed enjoyment which can be greatly assisted by a good technique. Those who read this book will have the opportunity to put this into practice.

1

TOOLS OF THE TRADE

There are so many variations in tackle available today, that even a very competent fisherman can sometimes be misled into parting with a considerable sum of money for nothing more than a splendid white elephant. The situation is far worse for the beginner who without experience on which to base a judgement can quickly waste a small fortune. It is all too easy to believe that a vast range of rods, reels, lines and accessories is needed to cover different waters and conditions.

Before giving way to any temptation created by clever advertising techniques, remember that the fishing tackle industry has to keep inventing new ideas and supplying a diversity of equipment to maintain profitability. This does, in fact, represent good business sense; it is also a challenge to the thinking angler who must sort out the good from the bad and the essential from the unnecessary. Unfortunately, an objective judgement on the necessity of a particular item can only be made by the more experienced fisherman who already knows what is really required to catch a trout, and who perhaps also has unpleasant memories of having wasted good money on mistakes in the past.

This chapter is to help the selection process, not by criticising all the bad and unnecessary tackle available, but from the more constructive angle of describing all the equipment which is actually needed — the armoury is therefore deliberately very selective, and is surprisingly small. We may be strongly criticised by those who maintain that a trout fisherman's degree of expertise is judged by his ability to utilise a wide range of equipment to optimum effect depending on the circumstances. In defence, we would argue strongly that being an expert means being able to adapt one's technique to the conditions, and that this does not require anything like the wide variety of tackle which many would assume. When we have been successful, both for pleasure and in competition, it has been with this narrow range of tackle, and on less successful occasions the failure has inevitably been associated with shortcomings in technique, misreading the water, carelessness, too much Rioja or Burgundy, even bad luck — but never inadequate tackle.

Expert fishermen may favour different types of tackle, to which we can only uphold our own ideas, and fly fishing would be a dull sport indeed if every-one agreed on the same tackle and techniques. There are always going to be

Using well-balanced tackle on the River Test

legitimate personal preferences. Most top fly fishermen, however, restrict their tackle to a bare minimum, at least in competitions where success matters most. This point is best illustrated by Bob Draper, one of the most successful fly fishermen of all time who represented and captained England year after year during the seventies and early eighties. All his fishing, from fly to live-baiting for pike, employed the same cut-down carp rod and a couple of lines. He more than any other firmly demonstrates that it is individual skill which is of paramount importance, and that it is possible to be extremely successful using very unsophisticated equipment.

We most definitely advocate a purpose-built fly rod for trout fishing, and would extend the range of tackle to more than a couple of lines, though nonetheless strongly recommend keeping to a restricted selection. Those wishing to buy additional tackle would be advised to consider the following questions before committing any money: first, is it a new innovation? And if so, would it not be better to wait until it has been tried and tested by others? At least one well-known manufacturer is known to put completely untried and untested tackle onto the market, backed by powerful advertising; but this is usually followed by withdrawal and leaves a large number of anglers out of pocket.

Second, is it produced by a reputable manufacturer who maintains consistency in his product range from year to year? Those marketing poor quality goods are forced to update a significant percentage of their range each season; one major manufacturer recently changed all its fly rods! Third, if it is associated with a well-known fisherman, is he recommending it because financially he is going to benefit, or does he really use the tackle himself? Some celebrities cannot possibly use all the equipment which bears their name, and one well-known rogue from years past recommended a rod design when he was offered financial inducement, which he had slated previously.

RODS

Materials Traditionally, all the best fly rods were constructed of built cane, and even today there are those who swear by the action of these for light line river fishing. On reservoirs, however, where line sizes tend to be geared more to distance rather than presentation, cane rods can be excessively heavy and put a lot of strain on the wrist, particularly after a full day's casting. The introduction in the sixties of much lighter, hollow glass-fibre rods was therefore a major and very welcome leap forward for the stillwater fisherman. Perhaps the most successful glass rod was the 9ft 3in Hardy Superlite which weighed a mere 4^{1}/$_{4}$oz for an AFTMA 7/8 line. Even some of the modern carbon-fibre rods are not significantly lighter than this, though the equivalent weight in a good design is typically about 3oz.

The next real improvement was by courtesy of the aircraft industry which played such a major role in the development of carbon fibre. Although carbon rods were extremely expensive and of variable quality when they first appeared in the seventies, technology and production techniques have improved to such an extent that it is now possible to get a good rod quite cheaply.

Although the individual fibres are very stiff, a whole range of different actions can be obtained according to the way in which a carbon blank is manufactured, from the softest of brook rods to stiff tournament weapons. As regards the design of rods, it is difficult to see room for any further significant improvement, yet the tackle industry is inevitably coming out with innovative materials or new ideas on overall design. There is already boron, Kevlar and even hexagonal-shaped cross-sections, and while there may be nothing intrinsically wrong with any of these variations, there is no reason to adopt them per se in favour of less complex designs. What matters is the quality of the end product, and this can only be judged by putting a line on a rod and giving it a day's trial on the water; it is not sufficient merely to wave a rod about in a tackle shop.

Carbon fibres are much lighter and stiffer than glass fibres. This enables a rod of the same overall test curve to be produced with a much thinner and lighter blank. The decrease in diameter leads to greatly reduced wind resistance while casting, and this combined with lightness results in increased sensitivity, and less wrist fatigue.

Action The other major advantage of a properly designed carbon rod — not fully appreciated by many fishermen, nor, unfortunately, by some manufacturers — is its improved damping characteristics. A rod which is well damped will return to its unstressed position after being deflected without subsequent oscillations. A floppy rod which continues to oscillate before coming to rest has not transferred its energy efficiently to the fly line, and as well as reducing the distance it can also cast a wavy line. The term 'floppy' is often incorrectly applied to soft rods; there are some extremely good soft rods available, but there is no such thing as a good floppy rod.

A soft rod returns to its unstressed position slowly, requiring the casting action to be slowed down correspondingly to synchronise arm and rod. Such rods are often criticised out of hand by those who do not understand the mechanics of casting, and this is where the term floppy is so often misapplied. The advantage of a slow (soft) rod is that it gives the caster a good margin in his timing, and he can therefore be more accurate. It is ideal for use with light tackle due to its intrinsic shock absorption, and gives a much greater sensation than a stiff rod when playing a fish, making even a small trout feel like a monster.

Stiff rods also have their advantages. Provided correct timing is achieved, it is possible to cast a longer line, and for this reason they are always used by distance tournament casters. The faster (stiff) action means that fish can be covered more quickly, lines can be punched more effectively into a wind due to the tighter loop, and there is also less time for an adverse wind to interfere with the backcast. Finally, it is capable of bringing a fish to the net more quickly, and this can be an asset, for the nerves if nothing else.

Length There is a wide variety of lengths and line weights to cover all trout-fishing tactics. Very long rods (up to 12ft) are often recommended for boat fishing so flies can be dibbled across the surface. But although a long rod is in principle capable of casting a line a great distance, the leverage is too much for most wrists to support for a full day's fishing; this loch-style fishing therefore involves very little casting, but relies on working the flies a short distance in front of the boat. Delicate presentation is required and in some instances, the ability to use the wind to levitate the line away from the surface. Not surprisingly the technique is usually associated with light lines.

Making full use of the rod

A short rod imparts very little strain on the wrist and therefore permits effortless casting all day long; it also allows fish to be covered with much greater accuracy. If the rod is too short, however, there is very little control of the flies in the water, and distance casting is impaired since the rod tip moves too slowly.

Line Weight Line weight is significant: most rods are specified to cover two line weights, based on the AFTMA scale which assumes that 30ft of line (including taper but excluding tip) is being aerialised. Most good carbon rods are able to span a few line sizes, but this does not mean that there is not an optimum combination. Restricting the discussion to weight-forward floating lines, a rod classified AFTMA 6/7 will probably perform best with a number 7, but very satisfactorily with a number 6 line; it will also probably handle lines rated AFTMA 5 and 8. Line choice is always a compromise, since a line should be as light as possible to land delicately on the water and to maximise the sensitivity to the slightest pull from a trout, but sufficiently heavy to have the inertia to overcome air resistance over the required distance, particularly in an awkward wind.

How much emphasis is put on distance as opposed to presentation varies with the method of fishing. Thus the dedicated loch-style fisherman will base his fishing around an AFTMA 4 or 5, the long-lining boat fisherman and the small stillwater bank angler round a number 6 or 7, and the reservoir bank fisherman round a number 7 or 8. Although beginners usually find it easier to start off with slightly heavier line ratings, aiming to move down with experience, it is arguably better for them to learn with the right tackle from the outset, and to build up confidence and techniques on smaller waters (but not to the exclusion of reservoirs) where distance casting is less important.

Choice Central to our discussion on fly rods therefore is the one word 'compromise', and this also dictates our philosophy on tackle choice. While each style is ideally suited to its own optimum rod design, most successful trout fishermen favour a rod which can handle all conditions and for which the disadvantages, as compared with having a specialised rod for each application, are marginal. It can be difficult enough during a day's fishing to decide on the location, line and fly without having the rod to choose, too. Furthermore, using only one rod makes changing tactics far less troublesome, and any rod which does not have the versatility to cover all stillwater techniques is not worth considering. Since our classification of fly fishing is largely based on international rules, tactics involving the use of large lures or trailing at depth behind the boat — which may require much more robust tackle — are not included.

Finding the right model may involve considerable trial and error which can be an expensive business. Once the right choice has been made, however, the temptation to invest in additional rods will evaporate, new innovations will be judged as interesting ideas rather than essential items, and from that moment on fishing skills will improve since the angler can now concentrate on tactics rather than worrying about inadequate equipment.

Casting So what is the first step in choosing the perfect compromise rod? The vital requirement is the ability to cast correctly, because even the best rod is hopeless in inept hands, and there is no chance of assessing the true characteristics of a rod unless it is used properly with the correct casting style. A surprisingly small fraction of reservoir fishermen can cast a fly efficiently, yet while prepared to pay £100 for a rod, few seem willing to part with half that amount for a couple of days' professional tuition. The average fisherman will cast much, much better with a £40 rod and a correct technique ensuing from proper tuition, than he ever will with a rod costing over £200 and incorrect technique.

Whether tuition is required can be assessed by asking yourself a few simple questions. Do I:

(1) move more than just my arms?
(2) often get the leader into tangles?
(3) have problems casting 25yd effortlessly?
(4) need to stand when casting in a boat?
(5) ever worry that I cannot cast as far as I ought to?
(6) control distance solely with my casting arm?

If the answer to any of these questions is yes, then there may well be a casting problem which needs to be rectified before spending good money on, perhaps, the wrong rod.

Good, professional casting tuition can be obtained from several sources, including members of the Association of Professional Game Angling Instructors. However, these casting instructors are not necessarily the best people to advise on individual rod choice or on stillwater tactics generally, particularly for the larger reservoirs. Pay your money and take advice on basic overhead casting technique, but leave your tactics and tackle selection to your own judgement (based, if you like, on the guidelines in this book). Rod choice is very subjective, and the only way to find out whether a rod is suited to any individual's style is to try it out, preferably for a whole day. This is rarely possible unless it can be borrowed from a friend, but events such as the Game Fair, and casting sessions organised by the larger fishing clubs often present an opportunity. Some manufacturers also have casting facilities where their rods may be tried without obligation (though beware of the temptation to buy on the spot).

Our Selection Our individual rod choices were the result of buying (and subsequently selling) many different models, but in each case the final version has remained the firm favourite for many years. JD uses the Lamiglas 9ft 6in AFTMA

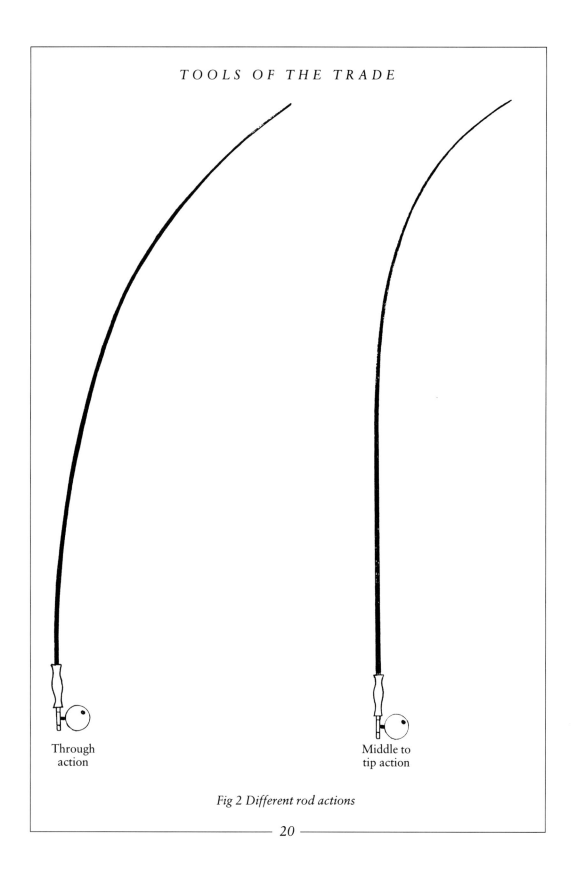

Through
action

Middle to
tip action

Fig 2 Different rod actions

6/7, which has a middle-to-tip action very similar to the Shakespeare Radial Nymph 9ft 6in 6/7 rod favoured by MC. Both rods are just stiff enough to let the angler dictate to the line, but not so stiff as to be unforgiving in timing or shock absorption. CO prefers the softer through-action of the Orvis Osprey, rated at 9ft 6in AFTMA 6, and the Drennan 'Oxford' series. These are slightly more forgiving for light line use than the other two rods but require a slower casting action. The rods vary in price from £40 to nearly £300, indicating that neither price nor manufacturer is necessarily a guide to rod choice. Otherwise, allowing for individual preferences in action, it is fair to say that these rods have a great deal in common, and this in itself should be a guide when choosing a stillwater fly rod.

First, their length is identical — this is no accident, since 9ft 6in seems to be the perfect compromise between control of the fly, accuracy, distance and effortless casting with the avoidance of wrist fatigue. Although loch-style fishing may not be very practicable with this length of rod, over recent years the 'Bristol fashion' of long-lining has generally paid better dividends. The point of a long rod in loch-style fishing is to be able to work the top dropper in the surface, but recently dry fly techniques have become very popular in stillwater fishing and these achieve the same effect far more efficiently. The emphasis for the successful trout fisherman should therefore be on effortless and accurate casting over reasonable distances (about 25yd). The line weight is also consistently chosen around the AFTMA 6/7 mark so, bearing in mind the wide tolerances of carbon rods, nearly all conditions can be covered.

One less obvious difference is that the Osprey and Drennan use hard snake rings, as compared to ceramic rings on the Lamiglas and Shakespeare rods. It is often argued that ceramic rings give a better shooting characteristic, but it is not always appreciated that this depends on the combination of rod and line.

LINES

Profile True fly-lines are designed for casting rather than trailing (or worse, trolling) behind a boat, and are tapered so they will turn over and present the flies delicately on the water — an attempt at casting with a level line will soon convince any sceptic of how important it is to use a line with the correct profile. It is sometimes possible to buy lines at bargain prices, and although they are often satisfactory, it is not uncommon to end up with an incorrectly tapered line which lands in a heap irrespective of how well it is cast. A good fly-line is a pre-requisite for successful trout fishing, and in the long term it usually pays to buy a top quality line from the outset. Bearing in mind the cost of a day ticket on most waters, paying £20 to £30 is usually cost effective if it will enable good presentation and consequently result in a high catch rate.

Take care not to buy unnecessary variations. It is very tempting to follow advice that a double taper is needed for presentation, a weight forward for compromise between presentation and distance, and a shooting head for extreme distance. While they do have these properties, to use all three line types will only add to expense, confusion and ultimate frustration.

Traditionally, fly fishing is associated with the double taper. The purpose of a taper at both ends is simply to allow the line to be reversed when one end becomes worn out. The line's major disadvantage is that inertia of the uncast section and friction from the large contact area with the rod rings, result in poor shooting performance. A considerable amount of false casting is therefore required to let out more line progressively to compensate for the lack of distance on the final shoot. However, false casting advertises the angler's presence and consumes unnecessary effort and time, so that flies are not in the water for so long, and there is an often costly delay in covering a moving fish. The poor shooting does, however, allow the line to turn over extremely well and to land gently on the water.

The most drastic solution to increase distance is to take the end 30 to 40ft of a double taper and attach it to some thin shooting line (such as 30lb nylon monofilament) which introduces negligible drag. In expert hands these shooting heads require only a single false cast and are capable of extreme distances. The problem is that thin monofilament backing is very prone to tangles and is easily blown about by the wind; thus, although a distance of well over 40yd may be possible, it may only be achieved once in several casts with the remainder ending in frustrating birds' nests. Furthermore, the lack of drag on the line gives poor turn-over, and to compensate it is essential to stop the line with the fingers just before the end of the shoot. Finally, very little 'feel' of the flies is obtained using a head, and this is something that can only be appreciated by experience. Perhaps

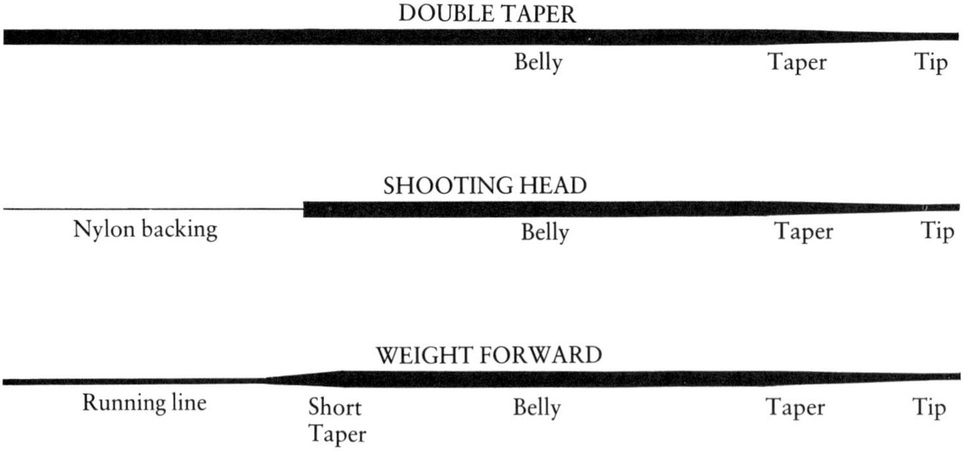

DOUBLE TAPER

| | Belly | | Taper | Tip |

SHOOTING HEAD

| Nylon backing | Belly | | Taper | Tip |

WEIGHT FORWARD

| Running line | Short Taper | Belly | Taper | Tip |

Fig 3 Line profiles

the most pertinent point to make is that nearly all the most successful fly fishermen have experimented with shooting heads and ended up discarding them.

The best line is the compromise between a double taper and shooting head. The weight forward (or forward taper) (which we employ exclusively) shoots much further than a double taper due to its thinner running line, but does not suffer from tangles or wind problems like a shooting head. Furthermore, in experienced hands its turn-over is not significantly inferior to a double taper, and a couple of false casts are all that is needed. It is therefore the optimum all-round performer for a relaxed and successful day's trout fishing, and the best advice is to ignore other types of line and join nearly all the best stillwater fishermen in restricting line choice to weight forwards.

When casting weight forwards, the length of running line outside the rod tip should be restricted to two or three feet before shooting the line. This prevents excessive line wear and gives better presentation, for the weight forward is not designed for aerialising much more than the 30ft or so of belly. In this respect the double taper does score, since any amount of line can be lifted off the water to cover a moving fish, although this advantage is qualified because the line will not shoot quickly to a fish at distance. Furthermore, with practice, considerably more than 30ft of a weight forward can be lifted off the water if necessary, though this should only be attempted by an expert caster when a fish needs to be covered immediately.

Sink Rates There are four separate line densities which are required to cover all eventualities. Number one in any fly fisherman's armoury should always be the floater, since for most of the season the fish are usually looking to the surface for food. A floating line can also cover a fair range of depths by using long leaders, making it extremely versatile. There are many excellent makes on the market, and it is very much a matter of personal preference whether to buy, for example, an Air-Cel, Cortland, Orvis or Masterline. It is important, however, to buy a well-established brand and in particular, to avoid lines with little or no stretch since they cannot absorb the shock of a savage take, frequently encountered from stillwater trout.

Next should be a very slow sinker; the fashion now is to refer to these as intermediates — which should not be confused with neutral density lines, designed to fish high in the water but sufficiently submerged to avoid line wake in calm conditions. Intermediates are truly slow sinkers which lie somewhere in sink rate between neutral density and that other well-known line, the Wet-Cel 1.

Intermediates have their place when the fish are lying a few feet below the surface and are not looking upwards for their food. Unlike a fast sinking line, they sink at a rate comparable to the flies and therefore do not force any unnatural downward movement on the artificial. Thus it is possible to fish very slowly and naturally while exploring various depths of water. They are particularly valuable

in early season from the bank, and throughout the year on boats or bank when fish are holding and feeding a few feet down, particularly in bright conditions. Their great advantage over the floater and long leader is that the fly is in direct contact with the angler, leading to more positive takes.

There are various makes of intermediate on the market, but JD and MC have no doubt whatsoever that the Wet-Cel is the best from every aspect. CO has always used his favourite Orvis which sinks more slowly, but this performs much better with the Orvis snake rings than with ceramics. The Wet-Cel is very noticeable by its colour, officially named Kelly Green — this does not seem to stop it catching fish, and there are those who think it may even have the reverse effect. Trout are curious creatures; for example, a lime green tag will often draw fish to a Stick Fly, and the Kelly Green could well have a similar effect in drawing fish to the flies. Speculation apart, this line sinks at just the right rate, lasts extremely well and performs beautifully.

Similar durability cannot be claimed for the Wet-Cel Hi-Speed Hi-D, but then this is one of the fastest sinking lines (capable of proper casting) currently on the market, and is therefore pushing fly-line technology to its limits. For boat fishermen it should be number two on the list of purchases since it is essential in early season to get the flies down to the fish. It also has its days throughout the season when the fish are holding well down, and it has often proved itself for bank fishing too, not just in deep water but when there is a strong cross wind which takes the flies round in an arc before they have a chance to sink to a fish-holding depth.

Due to its extreme sink rate, the High-Speed Hi-D places a very marked downward movement on the flies. Even when the fish are holding reasonably well down, they will not always be tempted by such an unnatural motion and the compromise under these conditions is an ordinary fast sinker. Although the Wet-Cel 2 is probably the most popular or best known, there are various other lines which are equally suitable.

The discussion on fly lines has been restricted to four different sink rates of weight forward, and there is no obvious need to extend the collection. It is true that a Wet-Cel 1, for example, bridges the gap between an intermediate and a Wet-Cel 2, but attempting to quantify the depth with such precision will only confuse selection on the day as well as increasing the expense unnecessarily.

To complete the choice of line, line weight should be mentioned, and in this case there is good reason for having two floaters. Presentation is of paramount importance when fishing the surface, and it is worth having a line one size lighter than optimum for flat calm conditions. This will also act as a spare, a very wise precaution (particularly in competitions) since lines do get damaged, and the floater is the one line which no fisherman should ever be without.

Careful presentation with a weight forward

The AFTMA rating specifies the weight of the first 30ft of a fly-line, excluding tip, and irrespective of sink rate. Thus, the greater density of a sinker compared to a floater implies a finer diameter and consequently less air resistance, leading to reduced loading on the rod. For an AFTMA 6/7 rod, for example, the perfect choice would be an AFTMA 6 or 7 floating line, an AFTMA 7 perhaps in intermediate and Wet-Cel 2, but an AFTMA 8 for the Hi-Speed Hi-D.

Line Colour One frequently argued feature of fly-lines is their colour. Brian Clarke and John Goddard's fascinating book *The Trout and the Fly* includes some very convincing photographs which attempt to illustrate why dark-coloured floating lines are much less visible to the trout. In practice, however, trout are seldom spooked by a line once it is on the water, but are easily scared by sudden movement which arises from the line in the air. Although an aerialised line is, to some extent, seen as a silhouette, it is arguable that light-coloured lines blend in better with the sky, and this theory is certainly endorsed by Mother Nature since many fish-eating birds have light bellies. Overall, the effect of line colour would appear to be very marginal — our combined experiences over many years have not produced any significant evidence in favour of either light of dark lines.

However, false casting can and does scare fish whatever the line colour — which emphasises the disadvantage of a double taper. Furthermore, fewer fish will be caught if the angler is unable to see his line, since slight movements of the line near the flies can often indicate a take which cannot be felt. When using a dark line the tendency is to lift off too soon when a fish is about to take, simply because it is difficult to see where the end of the line is in relation to the observed disturbance in the water. Use lines therefore which are easily visible — though there is no need to use grotesque glowlines which are available. For seeing the line on the water and for camouflage in the air, white appears to be a good all-round compromise.

LEADERS

There has been a great deal of controversy for many years on whether light nylon offers significant advantages in catching trout. Any experienced coarse fisherman will probably advocate very light lines for specimen roach for example, whereas large trout are frequently caught on very heavy nylon indeed. The confounding factor in trout fishing, however, is that a large fish is not necessarily well educated; besides which, double-figure rainbows are stocked in many waters as a matter of course — so care has to be taken when drawing any conclusions based on size alone. Most of our ideas on fly fishing quickly converged, but the advantage of light lines was the one subject which was not mutually resolved for a long time.

Now, however, we are all in full agreement: basically, there are many occasions when the fish are not put off by the strength of the leader at all, and ordinary 8lb nylon will catch just as many fish as the finest material. The heavier nylon has the advantage of being less tangle-prone and has a built-in margin against wind knots, line wear and 'smash takes'.

However, there are also many occasions when the fish are most definitely wary of the nylon, and it is not always possible to judge this from the conditions. Even when fish are being caught, there may be the suspicion that others are turning away due to their awareness of the leader. With practice, using fine nylon should present no major problems, and in fact it is a very good indicator of casting ability since a poor style is usually ruthlessly punished by tangles. The remedy is to try to cast more smoothly and gently; if this is unsuccessful, take expert advice rather than return in defeat to the heavier nylon. Fine nylon is usually most crucial near the surface, and if the fish are seen to be turning away, or if fish covered fail to respond even after changing the flies, try changing down. Quite simply, if nothing is being caught, there can be nothing to lose.

Double Strength Nylon Double strength nylon is an innovation which has revolutionised trout fishing. As yet it has only achieved partial success, probably because relatively few anglers fully understand its implications, and — more importantly — because they fail to use it properly.

During the winter months, we are lucky enough to be invited to talk to various fishing clubs around the country. This usually takes place as an open forum so that a two-way exchange of questions and views can take place, and the one that always gets asked, without fail, concerns leaders, leader rigs and monofilaments. This proves that most anglers realise the huge importance of terminal tackle, and the part that leader quality can play in helping them to catch fish.

Double strength nylon has in fact been around for several years now; the principle is relatively simple, but thanks to modern technology it represents one of the greatest advances in fishing over the last decade. In very basic terms, it is monofilament which in many cases has been pre-stretched to achieve twice the strength of conventional nylon of the same diameter. Theoretically, it should therefore be possible for anglers to fish with the same diameter nylon and enjoy added security and strength, or alternatively to fish much finer than normal without any sacrifice in breaking strain.

With fundamental advantages like these, how is it that fishermen are still using conventional nylon? Perhaps because the characteristics of the product make it behave differently and call for careful handling — the lack of stretch means that it is far less forgiving under sudden loads, so that 'smash takes' can occur much more easily; knots need to be chosen and tied with greater care, and the whole aspect of leader preparation needs close attention. At this stage it would be easy to become too technical, but the basic advantages of double strength are best discussed in plain English and then its merits examined in close conjunction with the actual leader rig.

Breaking strain When properly compared with conventional leader material, it is a plain fact that the breaking strain of most conventional monofilament is over-quoted. A leading German brand and its derivatives quote 7lb b.s., for example, when it will test up to 8lb; this practice leads to anglers becoming accustomed to stronger nylons than they *think* they are using. It is therefore more relevant to talk about diameter rather than breaking strain, as in any case this is more important in terms of what the fish sees.

Visibility On many occasions when trout have ignored flies on conventional nylon, we have changed to double strength and caught fish immediately — and this is never more true than when fishing a crowded area, when it can make the fish take the fly with much more confidence. If the nylon is less visible, then surely this must be the factor which is giving us more takes, when all other aspects remain constant.

There is absolutely no doubt in our minds that double strength nylon catches more trout. Equally, we have no doubt that if anglers do not learn how to handle it, then its benefits will continue to be under-exploited and even negated altogether. It is therefore worth looking at every aspect of handling in turn.

Success with double strength nylon on the River Test

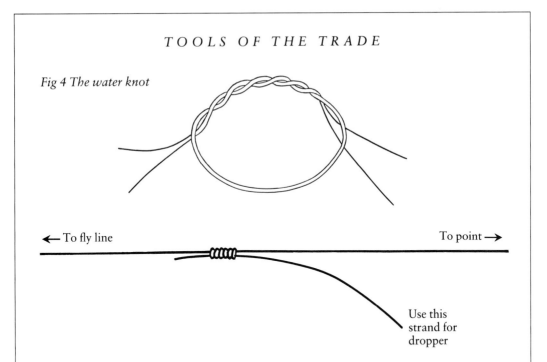

Fig 4 The water knot

← To fly line

To point →

Use this
strand for
dropper

Knots If knots in conventional nylon need to be tied with care, there is even less margin for error when using double strength due to its reduced elasticity and diameter. In both materials a Water Knot is ideal for droppers, providing the fly is tied to the strand pointing down the line — *not* the upward facing strand as is often so incorrectly advocated. Whereas four turns are usually employed for conventional nylon, three turns are more than adequate for double strength. For tying to loops, including eyes of hooks, a Single Grinner or a Tucked Half-Blood Knot is fine for both forms of nylon.

Care and attention Not all angling situations require the benefits of double strength, as in murky water or gale force winds the extra diameter of conventional nylon is not a problem, and can indeed be beneficial since it is less prone to tangle. It is in clear water, particularly when fishing on the surface, that double strength is supreme. You must, however, treat it with respect.

If a climber uses a thin rope and it becomes chaffed or damaged, it is considerably weakened, whereas a thicker rope can take chaffing with comparatively little reduction in strength. The analogy is directly relevant to an angler and his leaders, and it is a wise precaution to inspect leaders after every fish. The part most likely to be damaged is right next to the hook, and this should be retied after every second fish as a matter of security — this takes no time at all to do. Similarly, wind knots and minor tangles can weaken a leader construction, so reconstruct the leader every few hours. With practice this only takes a little time, but better still you can use discarded spools to store pre-tied leaders before you start fishing, storing them in a waistcoat or jacket pocket. For very little effort, these precautions will prevent unnecessary loss of fish.

Double strength has rather more shine on its surface than conventional nylon, and this should be treated as much as possible with 'mud' or Fuller's Earth mixes. Most fishermen use a leader treatment anyway, so with double strength it simply means that little bit closer attention to detail.

Leader rigs In recent years, dry and semi-dry fly fishing on stillwater has really come into vogue, and this style needs particularly close attention to leader construction and proportion. There are many national and regional preferences for leader configuration, but final set-ups are really a matter for each individual to decide, based on his own style of fishing.

The diagrams show the most popular variations, and one or two of our own suggestions. In all cases, we have assumed that the reader will be using a permanent butt at the end of the line. Our preferred set-up employs a braided butt section of about 30in and is shown in the first of these diagrams.

Using double strength should genuinely lead to better fishing and improved catch rates. The two brand names most worthy of consideration are Drennan and Orvis: they are both superb, and similar in all respects other than their colour. As

---

Fig 5 Standard butt rig – all lines
Fig 6 Typical Scottish/Irish leader for four flies.
It may sometimes be 'stepped down' in breaking strain, but is usually straight through at one strength. Advantages: simplicity itself. Disadvantages: unwieldly, flies too close, wind knots; very basic; unbalanced
Fig 7 Standard rig for double strength
The 5lb double strength is joined to the butt by a loop system, and not by a knot, as the diameters would not be compatible. This is the typical rig for a normal day's loch-style fishing. Lengths can be extended, but proportion is important. Advantages: balanced, with good turnover and good presentation. Disadvantages: too short for some wind/ weather conditions
Fig 8 Double strength rig for flat calms
A heavier tail fly should be employed for better turnover, either weighted nymph, or one tied on heavy gauge wire. Even with a floating line, considerable depths can be explored with this rig, and the confident caster will be able to increase the length of the tail section
Fig 9 Standard, single dry fly rig, using double strength. The tail section can be extended to 96in and still maintain balance
Fig 10 Hedged bet fly rig
This employs a very short 2 in dropper, with a small midge or sedge pupa. Fish often take this dropper, and the dry fly itself acts as a strike indicator. The length of tail section can be extended, depending on the capabilities of the caster
Fig 11 Double strength rig for semi-dry technique
Use a maximum of three flies for the cast, and again increase the length in proportion if you require a longer leader. All flies will fish in or on the surface. They will need to be visible to detect sipping takes, and as a consequence of this they need to be well spaced. The tail section can be extended depending on wind/weather conditions

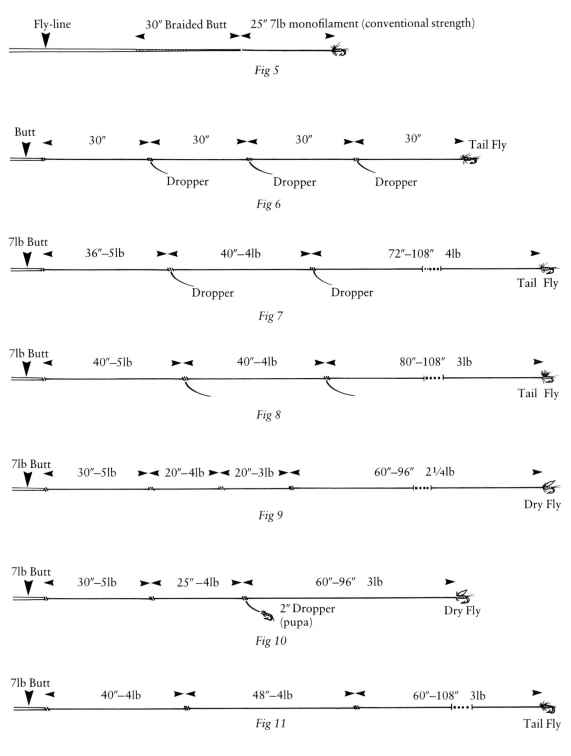

Fly-line   30" Braided Butt   25" 7lb monofilament (conventional strength)

Fig 5

Butt   30"   30"   30"   30"   Tail Fly

Dropper   Dropper   Dropper

Fig 6

7lb Butt   36"–5lb   40"–4lb   72"–108" 4lb   Tail Fly

Dropper   Dropper

Fig 7

7lb Butt   40"–5lb   40"–4lb   80"–108" 3lb   Tail Fly

Fig 8

7lb Butt   30"–5lb   20"–4lb   20"–3lb   60"–96" 2¼lb   Dry Fly

Fig 9

7lb Butt   30"–5lb   25"–4lb   60"–96" 3lb   Dry Fly

2" Dropper
(pupa)

Fig 10

7lb Butt   40"–4lb   48"–4lb   60"–108" 3lb   Tail Fly

Fig 11

part of your preparation for the new season, you could try the product for yourself; if you have already done so, try again on one of these rigs — if you did not realise the importance of knots and treatment, try them again. Your new season's fishing may throw you a very pleasant surprise.

Finally, in analysing the advantages of fine line, it is obvious that reduced visibility in the water plays its part. In this respect, colour is significant, too — anglers using dark nylon frequently obtain poor catch rates, and comparing dark and neutral coloured nylon in a glass of water should convince even the most sceptical fisherman never to use dark nylon again. Furthermore with fine nylon the fly is much freer to move about in the water in a natural, unencumbered manner. Without seeing through the trout's eyes it is impossible to assess the relative importance of the different effects, but the crucial point to emphasise is that fine nylon can do nothing but increase the chances of deceiving a fish into taking the fly.

Braided Leaders Just as a fly-line is gently tapered to achieve decent turn-over, so a sudden step down in diameter must be avoided when attaching the leader. This is not essential in practice when using heavy leaders (5lb ordinary nylon upwards), which can in fact be joined directly to the fly-line, but trial and error will demonstrate how turn-over falls off, particularly in a flat calm, when using lighter nylon.

The traditional remedy is to needle-knot a yard of thick (20–30lb) nylon to the fly-line, but thick nylon has a memory and the end result is coiling, which is far worse than using no butt section at all. The modern answer is braided leaders which have no memory at all, but unfortunately most manufacturers overdo the length of their braided sections. The length of braid should be kept as short as possible to assist casting short distances, judging where the flies are in relation to the end of the line, and casting into the wind. Although a braided leader may seem expensive, if connected properly it should last as long as the fly-line, and the capital outlay should not act as a deterrent for cutting it down to size. A good formula has already been shown in the diagrams.

Braided leaders in conjunction with light lines will also help shock absorption: however soft the rod, the drag of a fly-line in the water alone can sometimes cause the leader to break. The 'stretch' in the braid, however, occurs between the leader and the line, and in many instances can therefore prevent breakage.

The case for braided leaders with sinking lines is more debatable. The argument against them is that fine nylon and good presentation are generally not so important at depth. Furthermore, the braid will affect the sinking characteristics of the line, slowing it down considerably for a Hi-Speed Hi-D. On the other hand,

The importance of polaroids: with (top) and without (below)

there is usually the odd rising fish to cover immediately after changing over from the floater. Fast sinking lines in particular, having less taper from belly to tip, turn over less efficiently and in this case may benefit from the addition of a braided leader. On balance, therefore, it is difficult to make any firm recommendations for sinking lines, and the individual must decide his own priorities.

REELS

Reels tend to have a rather limited function. They play no part in casting because the line is always stripped off the reel beforehand, and when a fish is being played it is better to hand-line it in, rather than to wind up the slack and risk losing it due to lack of control. Even when the slack is recovered, it is not possible using even a geared reel to wind in quickly enough if a trout decides to head at full speed towards the angler (not an uncommon occurrence).

Automatic reels can recover line quickly enough to keep pace with a fast-moving trout, but they are so heavy that the luxury of being able to play a fish on the reel is of little significance compared with the unwelcome weight. It is also possible to slice through the backing line inadvertently with one of these contraptions. Altogether, they are best forgotten.

The purpose of the reel in fly-fishing is therefore simply to hold line. Occasionally a big fish will go on a long run, calling for reliability and a good ratchet to offer resistance and prevent the reel over-running and causing a tangle in the backing. To allow for a running fish, the reel should be sufficiently large to accommodate at least fifty yards of braided nylon backing. These features are straightforward, however, and can be found on the cheapest of fly reels — put any extra money into a comprehensive selection of quality fly-lines rather than buying an expensive reel.

A reel should be as light as possible. This assists effortless casting without fatigue, and increases the sensitivity to the action of the rod. Unfortunately, unless you are prepared to pay a large sum of money for excellence, such as the Orvis CFO reels, extreme lightness and good reliability cannot easily be obtained. Graphite reels may perform well in the shop, but on the water they soon stop running freely and are most definitely not recommended. The Ryobi magnesium reels are beautifully light (3oz) and run very freely, but with extended use they wear badly and the spool can become detached during use. The old faithful Rimfly is very well engineered for its price, but is perhaps a little bit heavy to be used in conjunction with lightweight carbon rods.

One way of keeping reel costs down is to use spare spools, but this is not ideal

Dean Hayes with a 4lb Rutland rainbow

since the greased parts of the spool are exposed so they collect dust and soil other items in the tackle bag. Reel choice is therefore very much a question of personal priorities, and our views do differ.

We all put lightness at a premium. JD uses the Ryobi 355 Mg, for which the relatively low cost means that a full reel is reasonably economic for every line. MC invested in the Orvis CFO; CO, as with most of his tackle, has always favoured Orvis. When all is said and done, though, reel choice is of only secondary importance compared with rods, lines and leaders.

BATTLEDRESS

Jackets Successful fishing is helped immeasurably by being dressed comfortably and having all the required equipment within easy reach. A good waterproof jacket is essential, and recently many new materials have been introduced to replace the more traditional waxed jackets which have inexplicably been the hallmark of fly fishermen for decades. It is truly amazing that in the modern age of spaceflight we should still be using an ancient technology which involves regular rewaxing — and waxed jackets are not particularly suited to fly fishing anyway. They have little resistance to fatigue, so that holes quickly appear in the elbows; nor do they 'breathe' particularly well, which is easily noticeable after being caught in a long downpour. We have all invested in modern substitutes. Without a doubt, wax-proofed jackets will soon be well and truly superseded by the modern breathable fabrics.

Trousers For bank fishing most waterproof trousers are adequate, but when sitting down in a boat the only suitable material to prevent a wet backside seems to be PVC or other plastics. No breathing material known to us can withhold the driving pressure across the seat of the trousers. The disadvantage is that PVC does not breathe which leads to problems with sweat, but currently there does not appear to be any alternative solution.

Waistcoats A properly designed waistcoat makes life very much easier since all the ancillary equipment is readily available — it is essential when moving about the bank or wading. It should hold a couple of fly boxes, spools of nylon, a priest, spoon, floatant, sinkant, scissors and any other small accessories; also that extremely useful bit of lambswool for holding and drying out flies. It is a good idea to use a lightweight priest and tie it by a lanyard to your waistcoat, since a delay in finding the priest is unkind and can result in tangles as the fish struggles.

Similarly, the spoon should be quickly to hand. Ideally, every fish killed should be spooned because this is the definite way to find out exactly what the fish have been feeding on; for this reason it is a good idea to have a combination marrow

JD in early season battledress with a Blagdon brownie

spoon and priest. Examining the stomach contents actually on the spoon can be very misleading; it is very much better to transfer them to a container of water where they spread out more openly and can be better observed. Unless this is done, small but essential details can be missed. A good example is the identification of buzzers — the right size and colour may be observed, but not the legs, so nymph fishing may continue when in fact the trout are taking the adult dry flies or perhaps the emerger.

Fly Boxes Many anglers take great pride in displaying huge selections of flies in enormous boxes. It may look impressive, and a great deal of satisfaction may have been obtained in developing such a collection, but it is not very practical. For a

Proof positive

start, the fly box ought to be readily available in a waistcoat pocket, and therefore must be reasonably small. Such a large variety also adds to the confusion of fly selection. Most top fishermen catch 80 per cent of their trout on a dozen or so flies, and the way they are presented should reflect this. We therefore adopt a two-tier approach: the twenty or so patterns which are either well established on their past performance, or are showing particular promise, are placed in the first box. The 'reserves' are those which may have only a very occasional use, or were successful in the past, or may be new ideas, and are stored in box number two. CO uses a further small box in competitions, for the successful flies from the practice day before, and for those which he would expect to catch fish with on the given water at the particular time of year. The whole philosophy is aimed at concentrating the mind.

The Wheatley (1602EF) 6in boxes with a centre leaf, and lined with ethafoam, are ideal for our purpose and hold a surprisingly large number of flies. Clips restrict the number of flies and can put the hook points at risk; they can also damage barbs and encourage rust. Compartmentalised dry fly boxes are a neat way to store flies, but take care that the lid does not spring open too quickly and distribute the contents at random.

Polaroid Spectacles The ability to spot fish successfully increases catch rates enormously — CO's excellent eyesight has undoubtedly made a significant contribution to his success. Very often a trout gives its position away by only the faintest break in the ripple, and such innuendos are virtually impossible to detect without polaroids due to glare on the water surface. Many fishermen only wear polaroids on very bright days for their own comfort, instead of wearing them (as they should) most times. Some glasses, such as Cormorant HLTs, allow much higher light transmission than normal polaroids, and should be the first choice for normal or dull conditions. A brimmed or peaked hat, pulled well over the top of the polaroids, reduces the amount of extraneous light and improves fish-spotting ability even more.

Spectacle wearers often avoid using polaroids since clip-ons can be surprisingly uncomfortable, but this undoubtedly costs a lot of fish. Try contact lenses, or order polaroid versions of normal glasses from an optician. Since such glasses cost about £100 there may be considerable reluctance to buy both high transmission and normal variations. The emphasis, however, must be on high transmission since the prime purpose of polaroids is to spot fish under all conditions rather than to act as sunshades.

Glasses have the further benefit of eye protection; they are therefore highly recommended on the bank and are absolutely essential in a boat — at dusk, when

CO with prize winning hat

even high transmission polaroids have to be removed, it is recommended that safety glasses are worn in the boat.

Nets Nets should be as large as practicable, a good design being triangular with 24in (60cm) arms. The handle should be light — many a good fish has been lost by the wrist giving way at the crucial moment. When moving around a lot, however, size can be compromised in favour of a net which folds and is easily carried at the waist, though choose a telescopic version since it is nearly impossible to reach fish from the bank with some of the standard handle lengths.

A net with a strong pointed handle is essential when wading. Not only does it peg the position, it can be inserted at an angle and used as a line tray. Some form of line tray is required to keep the line off the water, because the drag on even a floating line can reduce casting distances by several yards; on a sinking line, failure to keep the line off the water can be a disaster. Purpose-built line trays are undoubtedly effective, but we find them to be an encumbrance, and must also admit to the feeling of 'wouldn't be seen dead wearing one'.

Boat fishing is usually most effective on the drift. Even when the position of the fish is known, it is better to show the same fly once to a large number of fish than many times to the same one. Trout soon learn to ignore flies, and it is very common to see anchored boats picking up two or three fish very quickly and to struggle from then onwards. A drogue is a useful item for slowing down the boat, especially in a windstrength of force four and over; in other words, it is absolutely essential in a gale. It is unnecessary to use one in comparatively calm conditions, and can even result in lost fish behind the boat; it causes extra effort (and therefore resistance) when making minor changes in position to take advantage of local fish concentrations (on calm lanes, for example).

Bags Finally, it is worth having a suitable bag in which to prevent the fish drying out. Traditional straw bases are bulky, smelly and tend to disintegrate. Ironically, it is the traditional firm Barbour who have come up with a modern innovation using synthetic materials. Their bags fold up into tiny packages when dry and appear to be totally rot-proof when wet. They will last for a couple of busy seasons, especially if laundered for a couple of minutes (in a bucket, not a washing machine) after each day's use.

Bank fishing at Blagdon

2

THE TROUT AND ITS ENVIRONMENT

In formulating fly fishing tactics, success can be greatly increased by correctly taking account of the behaviour and environment of the trout, by appreciating his principal food-forms and the ways to imitate them, and by understanding how he may react under different water and weather conditions. The way he moves in the water may provide vital clues as to his diet, cruising depth and direction of travel.

It is not always a question of simply imitating the natural, because quite often a trout may respond more to a fly which stimulates his natural curiosity or aggression. This characteristic, as well as feeding habits, will vary between the different species and between residents and stock-fish, and quite different tactics have therefore evolved for the heavily stocked rainbows in many English stillwaters, compared to those for the wild brownies of Scotland and Ireland. Different tactics again may be required for small stillwaters which usually contain a greater percentage of stockies and 'spooked' residential fish.

All these factors have to be considered if the thinking angler wishes to understand *why* certain methods work better at some times than others. An improved understanding can ultimately only lead to one outcome — more consistent catch rates, since tactics will have been deduced from facts and logic rather than trial and error.

BROWNS VERSUS RAINBOWS

Brown trout are undoubtedly more difficult to catch than rainbows. On a size-for-size basis, a brownie will have lived for two to three times longer and will therefore be better educated. But the reason is more fundamental in that the brownie tends to be much more selective in its feeding habits, and can become more easily pre-occupied with one particular food item.

We sometimes fish a small syndicate lake which is stocked with both rainbows and fingerling browns. The browns very soon become pre-occupied with feeding on tiny dry flies, and once they have been hooked or pricked, they become very difficult indeed to tempt. No amount of clumsy casting seems to scare them, but it is a very fine angler indeed who can consistently deceive them into making a mistake — they seem to treat him almost with contempt, safe in the knowledge that they are far too selective to be tempted by his amateurish offerings.

In contrast, the wise old browns of the Itchen will disappear immediately on detecting the slightest movement from the bank. Perhaps we should say almost all, because there was one 2lb-plus aristocrat whom we tried to tempt for several hours. Cast after cast was made, and although he turned to investigate a dozen or so casts and came within a whisker of taking the fly on a couple of occasions, he was not going to be fooled. George, as we christened him, was so knowledgeable about what was and what was not natural food, that he no longer needed to dive for cover when fishermen approached. After all, why should he stop his feeding spree, just because of some clumsy angler? We admitted defeat, and dedicated this book to the fish who seemed to know more about anglers than most anglers know about trout.

Thus, tempting brown trout can be both fascinating and infuriating, as the darkest corners of the fly box are ransacked in search of a solution. This is a good experience for the thinking angler, for it forces him to examine all his ideas on flies, leaders and technique.

This does not mean that residential rainbows will snap at anything, since they too can be extremely difficult to deceive with artificial offerings. Their pre-occupation with a single food item does not, however, carry the same conviction. They are naturally more inquisitive than their thoroughbred cousins, and more willing to accept a varied diet at any given time. This, of course, makes fly selection much less critical.

It is the rainbow's inquisitiveness which makes him nomadic in his search for food — he will change location and suddenly appear, to take advantage of high food concentrations that have developed due perhaps to a wind change. The brownie, however, prefers to hold station in a chosen area of the lake that he knows from experience will hold a constant supply of food. Thus when fishing these areas, you are faced with a quarry that knows the local fly life intimately, and is a past master at spotting a fake, especially if it is moving too fast or is obviously the wrong size or colour. In most lakes these brownie haunts are usually well characterised; brownies tend to be higher up the pecking order than rainbows and will often see them off if they trespass too closely.

During the day browns will normally hold their station, but as night approaches they start to look around near the surface and move towards the bank. This message was first brought home to us when wading at Blagdon. After a tiring day, MC accidentally let go of the line on the backcast; the flies landed a couple of feet from the bank behind him, and were immediately intercepted by a brown of nearly 3lb — so our normal practice now is to cast out parallel to the bank in the late evening and early morning.

It is small wonder that the trout take advantage of the margins when the light fails, because this tiny strip of water offers safety during the day to any insect or

The gentle art of catch and release

small fish; since predators are frightened away from the bankside during the daylight hours, an abundance of food builds up.

Towards the end of the season, browns have a very strong instinctive urge to increase their food intake in preparation for the on-coming winter and spawning season. This drive can be so strong that they may lose their fear of man and gorge themselves in the margins during the day, a practice which is normally reserved for the evening. The margins are particularly productive at this time of year as the weed growth which has provided cover for the vast shoals of fry dies back. Fortunately, the end to the fishing season is timely and affords them the protection they so rightly deserve.

Fry form a major part of the brown's diet, and it is a spectacular sight to see the bigger fish charging through a shoal and scattering the fry into the air like a fountain. The fry are often not eaten on the first pass, but are left lying maimed on the surface to be taken as the trout return to mop up. Rainbows feed similarly on fry but to a far lesser extent.

The margins can tell us a great deal about the available food supply in the lake. If fry can be located close to the bank, it could be a good place to start fishing, because quite often they will have been driven there by the predatory trout which will be holding a short distance out.

Browns differ from rainbows in their reaction to changes in weather conditions, too. Any significant and sudden change will often send rainbows sulking down to the bottom of the lake where they may remain for several days before acclimatising. Browns, on the other hand, are the angler's favourite in such circumstances, being much more willing to continue with their feeding and therefore to rise to the fly — often in bad weather the ratio of browns caught is far higher than the seasonal average. On one infamous competition day on Chew, Tony Bevan won the coveted 'Brown Bowl' with a basket that contained five brownies — not a rainbow in sight. Perhaps when the sulking rainbows descend to the browns' normal depths, the browns simply dislike sharing quarters and move disdainfully higher in the water away from these unwelcome intruders.

Setting the hook in a brown's bony mouth can sometimes be a problem, even with the sharpest point. It is better to hook him in the more meaty scissors, and it is therefore often advisable to delay the strike slightly. This takes a great deal of self-control, and also a fair degree of certainty that the take will be a brown and not a rainbow. Furthermore, this question of delay is only a very rough guide, since there are many exceptions to the rule — on Loch Leven the browns will tend to hook themselves providing you allow them time to turn, whereas the slightest delay on Loch Harray or the Irish Loughs can be fatal. On most English reservoirs the delay should be pitched somewhere between the two extremes.

STOCK-FISH

Whether we like it or not, stock-fish are a fact of life on just about any British stillwater which holds rainbows. There are only a handful of places in the British Isles where this imported species can breed, and these must have the right conditions which include, above all, suitable running water. Even the most expensive beats on the hallowed River Test are heavily stocked, and fishing there can cost a hundred pounds a day for the privilege of taking a brace of stockies.

While most true fishermen would prefer to concentrate on residential trout, it is often impossible to avoid stock-fish. The situation is most serious for the small 'put-and-take' fisheries, because they have to stock on a weekly or even daily basis to keep an acceptable head of fish in the water. The better managed small fisheries take steps to minimise the problem. For example, Paul Knight at Steeple Langford deliberately keeps a large area in the middle of the lake which is inaccessible to fishermen. This establishes a good head of residential trout, and from time to time individuals from amongst these large and educated fish swim towards the margins and offer a real challenge to the skilful angler.

Since we will be faced with stock-fish even on the bigger reservoirs, it is worth

Andrew Donalson with a true Chew resident

understanding their behaviour. They are not always as easy to catch as many would imagine. Once a few of them have been pricked, the remainder can become very wary and be surprisingly difficult to hook and land.

Stockies usually behave in a similar manner on most waters due to the common rearing process. From a very early age to when it is released at, say, 1–2lb, a stockie's daily routine consists of swimming round the stew pond in a shoal, cruising the boundaries and nipping the tails of other fish. The highlights of its life are the feeding times which typically would be twice a day. Several fisheries hold these young in cages in the lake, and many wise old residents have learned that by living under the cages they too can get a regular supply of food. Recently released fish take some time to forget their feeding routine, and are noticeably up and looking for food at the same times in the open water.

Stockies will shoal in the lake as they did in the stew ponds, and patrol the perimeter, especially in winter. If their paths are known it makes a lot of sense to stay put, for sooner or later the shoal will arrive and the sport will be furious. In summer the shoals soon break up into splinter groups.

A sudden influx of stock-fish will disrupt the lake's daily routine, and tends to move the residents off-station. These fish, which may have been rather inactive, become much more vulnerable when stirred up and caught off balance, and it is not uncommon for the catch rates of resident trout to increase after a stocking. The phenomenon divides the anglers into two classes: the majority will follow the stock-fish, whereas the more initiated will take advantage of the dislodged residents which may have moved into casting range.

The situation may be reversed slightly towards the end of the season because the resident fish will by then be taking a more aggressive attitude towards the intruders. Instead of simply moving away themselves, they will tend to hold station and drive the stockies out of their territory.

Fish which have been in the lake for two or three weeks can be classed loosely as residents, since they will have started feeding on natural food items and have some idea of the differences between genuine and artificial offerings. When a new stocking takes place, these fish will tend to move away from the intruders; they will not, however, have grown full tails and in many ways will still resemble fresh stockies in appearance — it is therefore easy to be mistaken as to their identity and to form a false impression of the direction in which the new stock-fish have moved.

Unless conditions are cold when the newly introduced fish move down in the water, there is a tendency (but no more than that) for the fish to move upwind. Yet on Wentwood for example, the fish nearly always move away from the dam where they are introduced, irrespective of the wind direction. This is because they are introduced into deep water, and on finding a contour near the bank, follow it until it leads them to the shallower top end which has a good concentration of weed beds. In fact, the only reliable guide to behaviour is to record information in a diary over several stockings and to see if some pattern emerges.

The arrival of stock-fish into your vicinity can be quite obvious if you know what to look for. The first sign may be from the bending rods of nearby anglers, and it is not uncommon to see a wave of bending rods transmitted all the way down the bank. If you know the stockies' pattern of movement, position yourself at the end of their patrol, because they will remain longest in these areas. There are also spots on some lakes where two shoals meet and turn around, giving the angler the best of both worlds. Such hot-spots are often assumed to occur because of sub-surface features such as weed beds and ditches, but sometimes this is simply a whim of stockie behaviour.

The different rise-forms often give a clue to identity: the stockies' random dimplings tend to imitate a shoal of coarse fish, rising at anything floating on the surface; a resident trout, on the other hand, can usually spot the real thing from quite a distance away. And an inexperienced trout taking a small dry fly is usually a very noisy affair, with several attempts sometimes being made to secure its meal. Flies such as the G&H Sedge are probably so effective because their outline is very similar to a floating pellet.

Weighted flies such as Montana Nymphs (what a misnomer!) and Stick Flies

Stocked small waters are ideal for teaching the young

can also be very effective, since they are reasonable representations of sinking pellets. Thus the nymph fisherman will score using the same fly for both residents and stock-fish, and it is easy to see why the good 'percentage approach' fisherman bases his tactics around a team of nymphs.

Once stockies have been located, anglers frequently lose fish, and this is often put down to one of the greatest myths in fly fishing: the 'soft mouth syndrome'. Why a fish's mouth should harden a few days after being introduced into a lake is beyond our comprehension, but many fishermen blindly subscribe to this misguided belief.

Simple observation shows that many stockies are hooked just inside the centre of the top lip, indicating that they nip at the tail of the fly rather than turning on it and taking it in the scissors. Obviously, taken like this, the hook may only scratch the edge of the lip, or just penetrate the skin right on the edge so that it pulls out. This may be due to their previous habit of nipping tails in the stew ponds, or to nervousness after seeing some of their shoal pulled out of the water.

Whatever the explanation, this is their normal method of feeding, and the experienced fisherman will act accordingly; at all costs, the important rule is to avoid striking. This is almost impossible when fishing fast, but slow retrieves are usually much more effective, and they should be continued until the fish has actually turned on the fly and everything has gone solid.

The stockie soon learns to avoid lures and flies which are retrieved in a thoughtless, jerky manner — possibly having been pricked by an incompetent strike. He may still succumb to the same patterns being pulled back, as long as the retrieve is smooth and slow, and without the obvious danger signals, and may take very confidently indeed. In many cases there may be two or three fish following the same fly, and of course those which survive will learn to avoid the slow steady retrieve as well.

In this case the FTA principle will come into its own. The idea first struck MC when his fishing was temporarily disturbed by a large brown trout chasing the fly. Having stopped retrieving for a few seconds, he gave a couple of sharp pulls to straighten the line which resulted in a savage take. This was simply an example of the well-known sink and draw technique, and most fishermen will have connected with a fish in a similar way — though they probably do not realise how effective it can be to stop retrieving for a few seconds. MC made the whole retrieve less predictable, incorporating short jerks, long and short pulls and variable pauses. The effect on the fish was staggering, with four fish in the next four casts.

To confirm his theory, he took JD to the same venue the following week, and pulled out a couple of brace in next to no time. JD noticed the retrieve, but could not get it to work until MC gave the vital hint: 'Just imagine the fish following your fly, just like a cat watching a piece of string, and Fool Them About!' From that moment on, FTA became part of our everyday vocabulary, and it can be one of the most killing techniques available. It works best on an intermediate line, but its application is very general and not restricted to stockies.

On those occasions when the stock-fish have gone down, the obvious solution is a Wet-Cel 2 or Hi-Speed Hi-D line. The leader should be short — a few feet — to get the fly down as quickly as possible. The fish are most definitely not put off by the proximity of the fly-line to the fly, neither are they shy of the nylon. In fact it is not a bad idea to go up to 6 or 7lb breaking strain since there is only limited stretch in a short length of nylon.

If the fly snags on the bottom, it pays to use a very short leader of about one to two feet and a buoyant fly incorporating plastazote. In this case the line is cast out, allowed to sink to the bottom which will typically take two to five seconds per foot, and retrieved very slowly in two to three inch pulls. If there is no response, the leader should be lengthened by a few feet to allow the fly to float higher in the water. The fly is then retrieved so that it is pulled in one movement down to the lake bed and allowed to float up again for up to ten seconds. Takes can come at any time, but usually occur on a change of direction. The beauty of this technique is that most educated trout have seen, and ignore, flies being pulled downwards, but the few that have seen one moving upwards are now in someone's freezer.

One day during a flat calm on Rutland, we were surrounded by a very nervous

FTA from the boat

Brownie variations: Bewl Water (top) and Lough Conn (below)

Magic moments on Blagdon

shoal of stock-fish. By accident, when pouring a cup of tea after casting a Hi-D line out on a fifteen foot leader, we discovered that the rod tip moved in a way which reminded us of our coarse fishing days with quiver tips. This led to several fish in a short period before the wind increased, attributable to the belly of the line sinking in a 'V' shape and pulling the flies down in a very gentle trajectory.

The flies we find the best for stock-fish include sometimes a Viva, whereas at other times they really go for orange, or for an imitative pattern like a Stick Fly or Buzzer. A detailed fly choice, however, is deliberately not included because we want to emphasise very firmly that it is the retrieve which is of paramount importance.

It is worth trying to establish when stock-fish can be properly classed as residents. There is no fixed time limit for this transition, because the trout's progression must depend on his environment — he will learn by example from other trout, and in a fertile water this can be a rapid process because he will frequently witness the other fish feeding, and have plenty of food to experiment with himself. Once he starts feeding on the naturals he is again very vulnerable to the angler, particularly to the nymph — rather than the lure — fisherman. After seeing some of his shoal removed, and perhaps surviving a close shave himself, the stock-fish will become much more selective: at this point, whether he has grown a full tail or not, he will have earned his status as a resident of the lake.

On one occasion at Horseshoe Lake, we caught a stockie which was full of a mixture of pellet mash and corixae. On being released into the lake, these stockies had encountered a shoal of resident fish feeding close to the bank which were not going to relinquish their feast, and remained in position. The stock-fish were obviously quick to imitate the residents, and then both would only respond to direct imitations of the natural.

CHANGE DAYS

'Change day' is a term used to indicate a sudden change in weather conditions. It may be wind direction or strength, rain, sunshine or an overnight frost. There are many combinations of weather conditions which influence trout behaviour, and it is always worth logging any dramatic changes between fishing trips as this can provide valuable information on where to fish, or even whether to bother fishing at all.

Chilling of the water surface is usually brought about by a wind change, and our records show that any wind directions from the north, north-east, east or south-east must be treated with caution. The coldest winds will come from north and east, and even a moderate wind from this direction can give a chill factor which makes fishing virtually impossible. If these conditions persist, it can sometimes take up to two weeks before the fishing starts to pick up again, and then it may

A crisp winter morning at Langford

only be a half-hearted affair. Even if the bad weather only persists for a couple of days, it can still set the catch rates back by a full week. If fishing under such adverse circumstances, find natural cover from trees or bushes.

Frost can also send fish straight to the bottom of the lake. There will always be a few which continue to search for food, but it is a waste of time to fish on the top since the surface is constantly chilled by the air and is therefore unpleasant to both the trout and the pupae on which they feed. Pupae are known to rise in the water, but they also descend when encountering a cold layer, so even if the trout has acclimatised to the change in conditions, surface feeding may not occur if it is too cold for the pupae.

For most of the fly fishing year the south-west winds are prevalent, though they can swing anywhere between NW and SE (in an anti-clockwise direction). Our records show that a temporary swing from SW to NW for a couple of days can disrupt the fishing for up to a week, depending on the wind strength and time of year. A temporary swing from SW to W, however, will be less serious, having no effect in a light wind and only disrupting the fishing for a couple of days when the wind is strong. A rule of thumb we use for boat fishing on Chew is that if you need to wear a scarf against the wind, the fishing is likely to be difficult.

Variable winds can play havoc with feeding fish. For example, if the wind suddenly changes to easterly in the morning, fish feeding on the surface will find themselves moving upwind (as is their custom) into the sun, which will greatly handicap them in their efforts to take the fly. They are very often accused of coming short by those who blame the effect on the wrong fly, perhaps, or the leader, but trout do not like looking directly at the sun any more than we do — one way to overcome this problem is to hold the fly at the end of the retrieve which makes the fish swim across the ripple to take the fly, in a direction away from the sun.

When fishing with two in a boat, one angler will often have the greater advantage if the fish are moving across the waves to avoid the sun — if they are at his end of the boat he will obviously be able to have first crack at covering the greater number of fish. In a competition it is vital to recognise this fact; on a fun day, our usual tactic is to get the partner to consume most of the wine so that he either fails to notice or does not care.

Sometimes the glare from the sun across the ripple can make fish-spotting very much easier from one side of the boat; this effect can occur for varying periods of time during the day depending on the cloud formation, but it is always very noticeable at dusk. Protocol should be such that both fishermen share the same illuminated area.

PRINCIPAL FOOD ITEMS

Midges Midges in one form or another are probably the most important food item in the stillwater trout's diet. The larvae are the familiar bloodworm, often a deep red, although other colours such as green and brown are also commonly encountered. They are typically up to an inch in length and are usually found wriggling about on the bottom of the lake, although a good blow on the water — or even more effectively, the disturbance introduced by aerators in reservoirs — can deposit them helplessly in mid-water where they are at the complete mercy of the trout. Trout can sometimes become pre-occupied with bloodworm, and in some lakes they are the staple winter diet when other food-forms are scarce.

There are many artificials to represent them, and even some of the traditional buzzer patterns can be effective if tied very thinly round the bend of the hook. Such representations, however, lack the vital wriggling action, and a much better artificial employs a red rubber band or 'power gum', one end of which is simply tied on to a short-shank hook. Unless the naturals have been displaced upwards by water movement, this should be fished as close to the bottom as possible with very slow one inch pulls.

'So that's what they're feeding on!'

Fig 12 Midge larva (bloodworm)

When the bloodworm transforms into the midge pupa (the familiar buzzer nymph) it immediately becomes more accessible to the trout since it spends more time in open water with the occasional trip to the surface. Buzzers may often make several trips to the surface but fail to hatch because they encounter a chill which sends them down again. The colour of the pupa is usually darker than the bloodworm, and it has white breather tubes at the head and small wing buds over the thorax. As it approaches the emergent stage, it exhibits a silvery appearance from gas which forms between the body and skin; this increases buoyancy and helps the case to split so the adult can break free.

There are many favourite patterns for the pupae at this stage, usually incorporating seal's fur, wool or silk tied slightly round the bend of the hook with white wool at the front. More general imitative patterns, such as the Diawl Bach and Stick Fly, also work well.

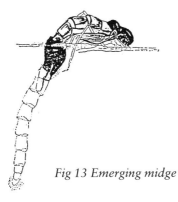

Fig 13 Emerging midge   *Fig 14 Midge pupa (buzzer nymph)*

Emergence usually occurs when the water is relatively calm and warm. The pupa adopts a vertical position accompanied by a wriggling motion. As the thorax splits, the emerging legs are employed to gain a grip on the surface film as the adult emerges from the now horizontal pupa. The wings at first exhibit a light orange colour before becoming transparent which accounts for the orange thorax in some buzzer patterns, as well as making flies such as the Dunkeld, Grenadier and Soldier Palmer so effective. Other more sophisticated emerger patterns employ a 'Ginked' or 'Permafloated' front end which rests on the surface whilst the untreated body dangles in the water.

Fig 15 Adult midge

Once the wings have been inflated, the adult midge stands on the surface film until his wings have dried sufficiently to take off. This is a very vulnerable time, since the trout is, in fact, very partial to these adult flies. Artificials include traditional dry flies and ordinary buzzer or hackled nymphs which have been 'Ginked' or 'Permafloated'. The next time the adult midges are seen is when they assemble in thick clouds close to the water; this is when they make the famous buzzing noise, although the 'buzzer' name is usually applied to the nymphs. This gathering usually takes place in the evening just after sunset when the hook-shaped adults return to the water to lay their eggs before they collapse spent, onto the surface.

Fig 16 Sedge larva (caddis)

Sedges The larva of the sedge fly is remarkable in that it builds itself a home in the form of a hard tapered shell about an inch long. Its popular name is the caddis, and it may be constructed from a variety of materials including pieces of leaves and stick, vegetable matter, sand and tiny stone chippings. Because of the materials available and the need for camouflage, these shells usually take on the colour of the surroundings. Tobacco is probably the most frequently encountered colour on our stillwaters, with green coming a close second, although sand and chippings are more commonly used in running water habitats, and provide extra weight for ballast against the currents.

The most general artificial pattern to match the natural is, of course, the Stick Fly. Peacock herl, ostrich herl or pheasant tail can be used to represent the body which should ideally be weighted or tied on a heavy wire hook. A fluorescent green thorax is often promoted as an imitation of the lighter head, but in reality this colour at either the head or the tail of the fly is probably used simply because it is known to be attractive to the trout.

The caddis transports itself by a cluster of legs protruding from the front of the shell at a rate which would make a snail look like an olympic sprinter. When fishing a caddis imitation, therefore, the retrieve should be extremely slow. Five to ten minutes per cast is still much too fast for the natural, but should be slow enough not to raise too many alarm signals to the trout.

Sedge pupae are generally in evidence from June onwards, and are noticeable by their well-developed wing cases and antennae. Their paddle-type legs make them good swimmers, with a jerky action making them instantly recognisable to trout and angler alike. There are numerous different colours, but the most common are amber, green and brown. Good artificials are the Amber Nymph and our own Green Panacea, fished on a floating line with a fairly fast and jerky retrieve.

Some species of sedge pupa hatch in open water, while others swim to the shore or weed beds. They are not observed in such large numbers as midge since their time of transition to adult at the surface is very much shorter. This often results in more splashy rises, as the trout has to act much more quickly to capture his food before it escapes.

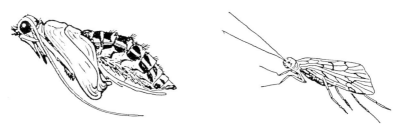

Fig 17 Sedge pupa   *Fig 18 Adult sedge*

The smaller sedges generally hatch during the day, the larger varieties in the evening; the Invicta or its silver variant are both excellent flies for imitating the pupa as it hatches into the adult. The adults tend to skitter across the surface, and it is not uncommon to see the trout chasing and chomping after them — this can give you a good idea of how to move your artificials. Good flies for such occasions are a Soldier Palmer and Wickhams Fancy (with or without its wings), and these should be well 'Ginked' or 'Permafloated'. These flies can be pulled quite quickly across the surface, but a static dry fly — for example our own Squirrel Sedge — can also be very effective.

Damsels The damselfly is most obviously important to fishermen because it is big, up to an inch or more in length, and something so large is obviously attractive to the trout since he has to expend less energy in catching a single meal — one

Success during a hatch of sedge

damselfly can be equivalent to upwards of twenty midge pupae. Furthermore, the nymph is a very agile insect enticing the trout with its wriggling, thrashing movement as it propels itself through the water, resembling at times a small fish or even a newt rather than the nymphal form of a fly. It is probably this movement which sometimes causes the very splashy rise-form which can easily be misinterpreted as fry feeding.

There are two stages in the damselfly's life-cycle which are relevent to the angler: the nymph and the adult. In middle or late May, depending on the weather and water temperature, the first damsels begin to appear. Rather like sedges, they tend to favour areas such as bankside reeds or stones, embankments and boat landing stages — not open water, since at hatching time the pupa needs an exposed feature like a reed stem to crawl from the water. It will crawl up the reed stalk and remain motionless for a few minutes while the sun plays on its skin (the shuck), which then splits as the adult insect starts to emerge. Front legs appear first, dragging behind some crumpled little appendages which could hardly be called wings. The adult will then crawl from the shuck, climb a few inches up the stem, and sit there seemingly exhausted by its efforts. The wings will gradually start to strengthen as blood is pumped into the veins, and assisted by the sun, will change from tiny tissue fragments into the beautiful transparent gauzy wings of the adult. A few minutes later the insect will launch into its first flight.

The nymph is several times more important to the trout than the adult, quite simply because in the water it is more accessible. Although there used to be speculation as to whether the adult damsel is actually taken, we have found them in many spoonings of both browns and rainbows; those blue slender bodies are quite unmistakable. We have also observed brownies at Lower Moor jumping out of the water to take paired adults, as the male carries the female low over the surface.

Damsel nymphs will be available from mid-May virtually through to the end of the season, and are most prolific from June to mid-September. Because they are so agile, the angler should never be afraid to employ a wide variety of speed and movement, and it often pays to experiment with both weighted and unweighted forms. Anglers who are used to a slow, steady figure-of-eight retrieve would do well to broaden their horizons when fishing the nymph — movement is the key, with the actual retrieve being as varied as your imagination will allow. Anything from a 2in to a 2ft pull can be effective, and by shortening the leader on a floating line, deep holes between weed-beds can be fished with minimum risk of snagging.

As in any fly fishing situation, a stealthy approach is required and watercraft is at a premium: avoid ploughing through bankside rushes with size ten waders, and concentrate on the shallow margins where the fish will be feeding quite contentedly unless disturbed. Trout will often take damsel nymphs in remarkably

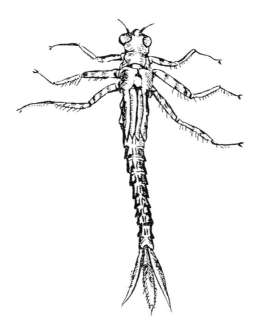

Fig 19 Damsel nymph

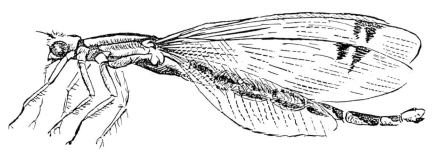

Fig 20 Adult damsel

shallow water, so the rule is simple: fish your way through the margins and rushes, and always expect the unexpected.

Fishing the adult insect is much more of a challenge, and requires a complete change of tactics. The adult is only available to the trout firstly, when it climbs down the reed stalks to lay eggs; secondly, when it occasionally flies too near to the water surface and becomes waterlogged; and thirdly, when it is taken in mid-air — imitating this must be the ultimate test of any fisherman who is prepared to accept the challenge.

Corixa It is one of the inconsistencies of fly fishing that the *corixa* is universally known by its Latin, rather than its common name — midges are not *chironomids*, nor are 'snails' *gammarus pulex*, and anyone would have considered 'lesser water boatman' a perfectly satisfactory name; but everyone calls the thing a corixa.

Although present for the whole year, corixae will spend their time living contentedly among the weed beds until well into June. On most stillwaters, in most parts of the country, two things then begin to happen: the water level falls, and the weed beds begin to break up.

The drop in water level is important to the angler, because it usually enables him to fish through and beyond the weed beds — on Chew and Blagdon it actually increases the amount of bank available for fishing as the impossible withy beds are left high and dry, and areas that are unfishable at high water become hot-spots.

Marginal weed growth also begins to break up after high summer in most reservoirs. Shallower, silty areas of the lake are often the most fertile and will therefore be most favourable for weed growth. As the level drops, more clay is revealed, covered with the sparser blanket weed which degenerates from July onwards. Both these factors are significant to corixa fishing: the insects find themselves with less and less cover and so they have to forage more actively to feed themselves. The problem for them, and the good thing for us and the trout, is that this time of activity, profusion of numbers and minimum cover all seem to coincide.

Corixae are prolific feeders and extremely good travellers, colonising any new stretch of water within days of it being formed, and the remarkable fact is that they can fly just as well as they can swim. Indeed, it must be one of the wonders of nature to see an insect that lives on a lake bed swim strongly through the water, propel itself to the surface with those custom-built miniature paddles, and then break through and take to the wing.

This phenomenon takes place every year on Chew and Blagdon, and is truly a fascinating sight. The versatility of the insect is incredible, and on many occasions we have made a grab at one as it flies past to try and examine it — if it is knocked onto the water it instantly becomes aquatic again, diving to the bottom as though it had never been in the air.

An understanding of how and when an insect moves and lives is paramount in knowing how best to imitate it and fish with it. Only the adult stage in the corixa's life cycle is relevant to us and the fish — the bonus is that the adult is easy to represent at the tying bench. In its continual search for food, it makes repeated trips to the water surface to replenish its air supply. It carries this to the bottom in the form of a tiny air bubble which shrouds its body, held in place by microscopic hairs and its own tension — any artificial should really incorporate a silvery sheen to represent this feature.

With all that buoyancy, corixa obviously has to work hard on the descent, with paddles struggling furiously. Thus more important even than the tying, is the way in which the artificial is fished. Ideally, all corixa patterns should be weighted, otherwise it is impossible to imitate the jerky ascending and descending movement of the insect as it replenishes its air supply. A 6 to 8ft leader length is sufficient for corixa fishing, and a floating line is first choice since the insect inhabits shallow areas where an ideal fishing depth is about 4 to 5ft. On Blagdon in particular, Top

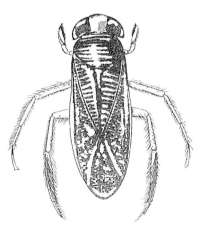

Fig 21 Corixa

End is the place to be from July through to September: the whole area is very shallow, yet because of the feeder streams, the fish tend to congregate here for the final big feed before autumn. Spooning captured fish will invariably reveal hundreds of corixae, often to the exclusion of anything else.

The simplest and most effective method of fishing the artificial is to watch for moving fish and throw the corixa about a yard ahead. A well-leaded fly will sink around a foot in a few seconds, and a long draw to lift it to the surface should provoke the appropriate reaction from the fish. Even so, the trout will often be feeding on the corixae sub-surface and so a longer pause will be needed after casting to allow the fly to sink. The value of a short leader now becomes apparent: anything longer than 8ft will result in too shallow a climb, as the naturals tend to rise almost vertically. A lot of takes will come 'on the drop', and of course this is a fair representation of the diving insect. If nothing is showing at all, it is worth prospecting the shallows either with a swift figure-of-eight retrieve, or in sharp pulls of 6 to 8in at a time.

Unlike some nymphing methods, corixa can and will fish effectively from a boat. A drift over the shallows, short casting with a leaded artificial and taking a lot of time over the lift-off usually bring success, and this is particularly true of large areas of shallow water which are undisturbed by wading bank anglers,

Applying side strain to keep the fish clear of weeds

where the fish will be feeding at their leisure and where the cautious use of oars will be repaid many times over.

The corixa is an all-round insect which provides marvellous late summer sport. It is the most versatile and highly mobile, able to change its environment and move from water to air and back again at will, a remarkable feat in itself. It is available to trout in such profusion that the lake bottom often appears to be crawling; but above all, it offers the angler some of the most exciting sport of the year, with a fishing method uniquely its own.

Daphnia If you were to ask ten anglers about daphnia, maybe one would know how to tackle them properly. Some would say that the fishing was impossible, some would even talk about trying to imitate them; others would see fish feeding and yet not realise that the food-form was daphnia. This was really brought home to us when a highly respected international fly fisherman was heard explaining to an audience how the fish were feeding on tiny buzzers; if he had only spooned the fish he had caught, he would have seen that they were stuffed to the gills with daphnia.

We have also sometimes misread the situation, but if fish are spooned as soon as they are caught, the error should be rectified after the first fish. The trouble is that this first fish can often be very elusive if the wrong tactic is employed, so if covered fish repeatedly fail to respond, a daphnia-type approach should be tried.

Daphnia are very small crustaceans no bigger than a pin-head, but they are of prime importance to the trout and on some waters are the principal source of food — at Grafham for example, some of the phenomenal growth rates recorded in the past are due to daphnia. Their colour varies from greenish-white to orange-brown, and when massed together they form rafts of a jelly-like consistency.

Furthermore, daphnia are available to the trout for much of the year and when other food is scarce, it is fair to say that if you can locate the daphnia, you have found the fish. Daphnia near the surface are quite easy to see especially in clear water, forming oily slicks which are usually fairly dense. Even when they are lying deep, the angler has a good idea where they will be, since they are at the mercy of the winds and currents and will be blown towards the downwind shore. The best catches of trout in the early season therefore often come from these areas, which is why the east shore at Chew can fish so well in the opening week. The fishing on a downwind shore at this time of year can also be greatly assisted by thermoclines, in which the warmer surface water is driven by the wind and congregates at this end of the lake.

The depth of daphnia in the water depends on the light conditions; they generally remain near the surface when it is overcast, but migrate downwards in bright sunlight. Therefore catch rates may dwindle when the sun comes out, but exploring the depths with sinking lines can remedy the problem.

It is obviously a complete waste of time trying to imitate a daphnium, since even a good imitation (which would have to be very small indeed) would stand little chance of being taken among the millions of naturals. Fortunately trout which are feeding avidly on daphnia will usually grab any brightly coloured lure or fly with confidence. Orange and lime green are particularly effective, and patterns such as the Whisky Fly, Leprechaun, Christmas Tree, Viva and Dunkeld will all succeed.

The key to success is obviously distraction, and there are slight differences of approach depending whether the fish are high in the water. Surface feeders, travelling upwind with their backs out of the water and their mouths open, and scooping up great quantities of daphnia, have a tiny field of vision so it is best to pull a brightly coloured fly right across their noses. For some reason, orange and red flies seem to work much better than green patterns high in the water. One ploy is to 'Permafloat' or 'Gink' a buoyant fly such as an Orange Muddler, which will keep the distraction high in the water and add vibration; if the trout are further down, the best approach is to fish a 'puller' such as a Peach Doll or Viva on the point, but to include an imitative or suggestive fly such as a Pheasant Tail or Dunkeld on a dropper. It can be surprising how often the trout will take the more natural fly in favour of the lure, although taking the lure off the cast will reduce the catch rate dramatically.

One of our early experiences was particularly interesting. We were fishing Chew from the boats in late April with only the odd fish moving. Suddenly there was cloud cover, and out of the blue, fish were swimming through the ripple. Had we been more experienced at the time, we would have realised that such a dramatic change in the number of fish as soon as the sun was obscured was most probably due to daphnia rising in the water — but we made the common and erroneous assumption that we were witnessing a buzzer rise. Fish after fish was covered until, out of sheer desperation, we decided to rip a Viva and an Orange Muddler through the water. Six trout came to the net in quick succession, but rather strangely all of them had taken the Grenadier which had been left on the middle dropper. The sun then came out again, but by now we had spooned the fish and therefore understood the problem, and continued catching on sinking lines.

The bright flies had obviously distracted the trout, but the question remains as to why they all took the Grenadier. We maintain that the Viva brings out the aggression in trout, and in this case they may have seen it as a competitor for the Grenadier and accepted the challenge. The way in which brownies and rainbows react is very different, and we have often experimented with a fly such as a Dunkeld ahead of the Viva on the cast. With amazing regularity the brownies seem to attack the Viva directly, whereas the rainbows will take the Dunkeld from under its nose.

Once daphnia are located they must be followed with the wind; a sudden change in wind direction can change a hot-spot from one shore to another in a matter of hours. We have had many experiences at Rutland, for example, where a wind change has moved fish across the basin area from the dam to Normanton

Church or to Syke's Lane (and vice versa). It is counter-productive to have pre-conceived ideas on fish location from a previous day's fishing, but if daphnia are the main source of food, a wind change will invariably take the fish with it. Spooning is often regarded as a method of deciding on the correct tying of the artificial to match the natural, but with daphnia on the menu its main purpose is to give a clue on where to find the fish and its importance cannot be over-emphasised.

RISE FORMS

Consistent success in catching trout requires that as much as possible is deduced from the available evidence. Most emphasis is usually directed towards matching the artificial to the observed natural and on how to present it to the fish. However, one of the most obvious and neglected clues is the type of rise form left behind by our quarry.

Rise forms usually indicate trout taking food from or close to the surface, but not always; the inability to identify different rise forms can lead to many frustrating and blank days. Careful observation, however, can provide essential clues into the diet and depth of the feeding fish, and correct interpretation of the evidence can remove much of the guesswork out of fly fishing, and can increase catch rates enormously.

Rise forms may be conveniently divided into five main categories: the sub-surface boil, head and tailing, nebbing, sipping (or dimpling) and fry-bashing. Each will be discussed to help identify some of the signs and how to apply them to choose an artificial, then employ it to optimum effect.

The Sub-Surface Boil This is a heaving or flattening of the surface without anything actually breaking through, caused by a trout turning quickly to intercept food at some distance beneath the surface, typically one to two feet down. The most probable food is either buzzer or sedge pupae which frequently make more than one journey towards the surface and fall easy prey to a hungry trout.

Once a sub-surface boil is identified, there are further decisions to be made. Are the pupae hatching, or are they merely becoming active and making exploratory journeys upwards? Is it possible that the pupae are turning back because of a cold layer of water at the surface? When the air temperature falls below the water temperature it cools the surface; it is quite easy to check simply by putting your hand (which has become acclimatised to the cold air) in the water, where it will feel relatively warm. In this case the pupae are probably being taken by the trout on their slow descent after encountering the chilled surface.

To deceive the trout it is important to imitate the action of the pupae — in addition to choosing the correct artificial, of course. This involves selecting the right size, colour and shape of fly as well as the appropriate weight of hook. The fly

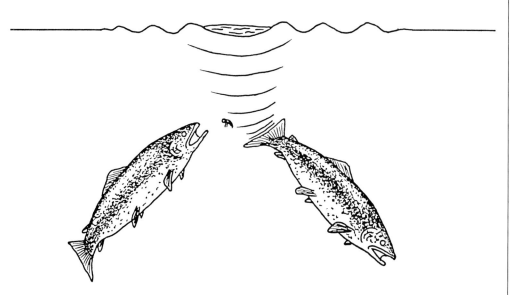

Fig 22 The sub-surface boil

must be presented at the trout's feeding depth, and the conditions described would be ideal for the intermediate line. Casting must obviously be accurate, and sufficient time allowed for the flies to sink; observe the line very carefully, since the trout are just as likely to take when the flies are sinking as when they are being retrieved.

Find the correct depth by experimenting in the margins — cast a yard or so out, count the time for the flies to sink a foot, and double this count before starting the retrieve when fishing. The line should be recovered slowly, with intermittent pauses to simulate the erratic progress of the pupae to the surface.

Head and Tailing This distinctive behaviour occurs when the pupae are hatching (as illustrated in the diagram) and the trout is swimming high in the water, taking food which may be on or just under the surface, or trapped in the surface film. To maintain his feeding position he must constantly head and tail, so his field of view close to the surface is very restricted, making him notoriously difficult to catch. Intercepting a cruising trout with a perfectly timed and accurate cast is easy to imagine but difficult to achieve in practice, particularly in an awkward wind.

There are four main food forms which will cause a trout to head and tail: snails, daphnia, caenis and buzzer. The first two are difficult to spot as they are entirely aquatic, whereas the others are visible as they hatch from the surface — the absence of caenis or buzzers would therefore point to snails or daphnia.

Snail migration usually takes place towards the end of the season over a comparatively short period, and can be very difficult to identify — it is easy to be taken by surprise at first. Once identified, a team of three floating patterns should be fished with a slow, steady retrieve. This is very effective when casting across the wind, allowing the bow in the line to move the flies for you.

Daphnia and caenis, on the other hand, need a different approach. The most effective technique is to use lures to distract the fish from its pre-occupation with these minute food items. Hot orange and fluorescent lime green lures work extremely well in the case of daphnia, and black lures such as the Viva are effective for caenis which hatch out mainly in the evening. The lures should be cast out as close as possible in front of the fish, and pulled quickly away to induce a take.

Unlike daphnia and caenis, buzzers close to the surface can be imitated easily by taking advantage of the lightweight Kamasan B400 size 12 hooks. A team of three buzzer pupa patterns with seal's fur bodies is used, and it is a good idea to treat the bob and point flies with floatant to keep them in the surface film, while allowing the middle dropper to sink slightly. The buzzers are fished almost statically with a very slow figure-of-eight retrieve simply to mend line.

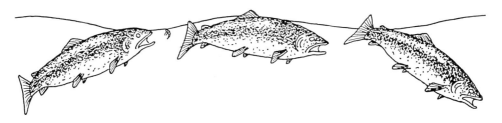

Fig 23 Head and tailing

The Nebbing Rise In this rise only the neb (or nose) of the trout breaks the surface, and usually occurs when a trout takes an adult fly on the surface or a fly which is in the process of climbing through the surface film. The amount of disturbance depends on the type of food being taken — usually the food is static and not likely to escape, so the rise is a leisurely affair.

Crane flies blown on to the water are sometimes taken with a loud sucking noise, as are sedges, and newly introduced stock-fish will also show noisy relish when they begin to take a fancy to the natural fly; the more experienced residential fish will feed quietly and confidently.

The procedure for dealing with this form of behaviour is, of course, the dry fly, and is a subject which could occupy the rest of this book; however, today's stillwater fishing techniques have taken much of the mystery out of dry fly fishing. The old patterns with their heavily tied wings and Metz hackles have given way to much less complicated flies with simple bodies of seal's fur or wool. The artificials are made to rest on the surface film by using water repellant mixtures such as Gink

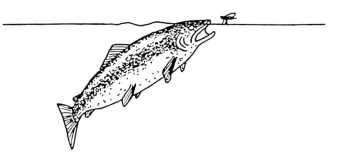

Fig 24 The nebbing rise

or Permafloat, and every angler should have some of these patterns (see page 110).

River and stream fishing still demands that more exacting profiles are tied to traditional styles with wings and tails. This is not really surprising because these trout see a constant supply of natural floating insects, and poor imitations can be spotted and rejected immediately without moving off station. Stillwater trout, on the other hand, generally go for much longer periods between seeing natural food on the surface and so are more readily seduced into taking an inexact artificial. These floating artificials often lose their attraction as a rise gets underway, reinforcing the comments about river trout being very adept at spotting fakes. However, the stillwater trout also learns to identify the differences all too quickly, though as the food supply starts to wane, crude fur and wool patterns fortunately start to regain their effectiveness.

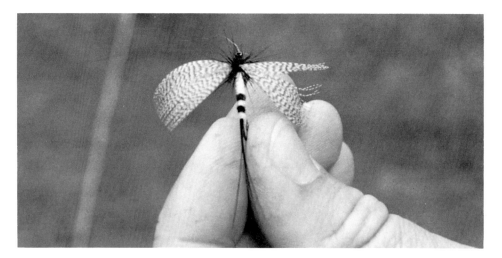

A more exacting profile for river fishing Graham Hadlow's mayfly

The Sipping or Dimpling Rise This is without doubt the most confusing rise form. Not only are there many different varieties of food which prompt this manner of feeding, but the direction of the trout is also very difficult to plot, although by studying the rings created by the rise, it is possible to establish this with a fair degree of success.

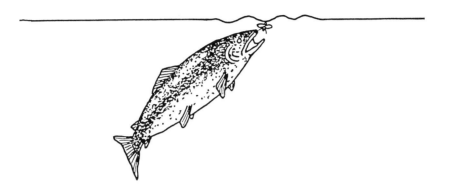

Fig 25 The sipping or dimpling rise

The trout's cruise depth can also be estimated by looking at the ring formation. As a very rough guide, trout cruise at a much greater depth in clear waters; their window of vision of the surface is greatly increased at depth, but they cannot take advantage of this phenomenon if the water is coloured because the light is filtered over a short distance which reduces visibility. It follows that the fish will make a bigger disturbance when rising from depth than if cruising near the top of the water.

A trout cruising at a high level will rise as shown in the diagram, and the rings will be closer together on one side simply because he is moving in that direction. This rule breaks down when the rings on the side with the greater spacing are seen to bulge. In this case the trout has come up from a greater depth and displaced more water with its body. This, added to the thrust from its tail when diving down again, increases the size of the rings and makes them bulge in the direction in which he is travelling. In some conditions it may be necessary to squat down slightly to see the bulging profile.

We first deduced the bulging ring phenomenon when observing trout from a high vantage point at Wentwood reservoir in South Wales. This is a lake set in beautiful surroundings with very clear water, and the fishing here improved out of all proportion when a local club took over the management of the fishery from the Water Authority. On this particular occasion our success rate in trying to predict the position and timing of the next rise was very low, far lower in fact than we would have achieved from random guesswork. This indicated some definite

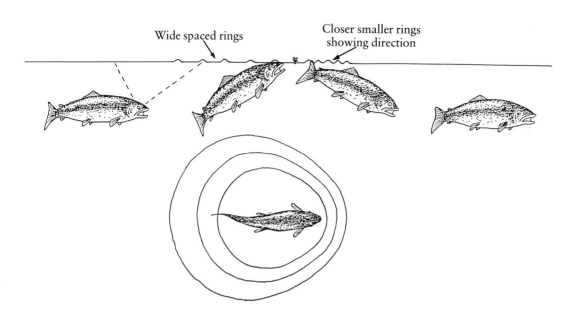

Fig 26 The surface cruiser (non-bulging rings)

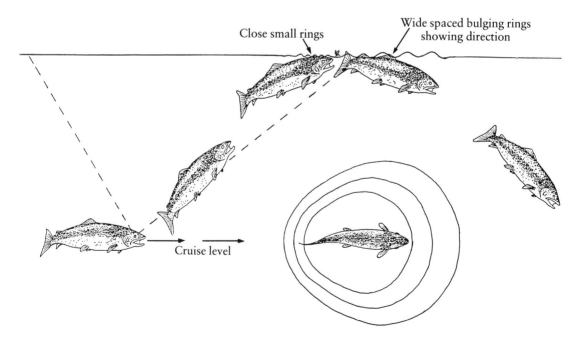

Fig 27 The deep cruiser (bulging rings)

Wentwood Reservoir – overlooking the valve tower

systematic effect which we did not understand, and we were therefore determined to investigate why our simple rule of direction deduced from close ring formation on one side of the rise form was not working on this occasion.

Firstly, we realised that most of our predictions were a full 180 degrees out; and second, we noticed that the distance between rises was significantly longer than usual. The final key to unlock the puzzle came from the observed bulge in the rings which seemed to indicate that the trout were rising from a considerable depth. We deduced that this was associated with the higher water clarity, since the trout could take full advantage of the good visibility to increase their surface window in the hunt for food. There was also an indication that the food supply at the time was rather limited, because the trout were having to scan such a large area.

The simple rule of thumb is to cast in front of any bulging rings, if they exist, but otherwise to cast in front of the closely spaced rings.

So now we have a method of determining not only the trout's direction of travel but also his cruising depth, and it only remains to discover what he is taking. Since this rise form is usually associated with a flat calm or light ripple, the sipping sound suggests that the food is trapped in the surface film — it is often spent flies or empty shuck cases, and it is worth emphasising that a trout will very often take the trouble after a rise to 'collect the empties'. His progress will be slow and unhurried as his prey is, of course, unlikely to escape. The cast of floating buzzer and emerger patterns should therefore be presented in front of the fish in a static manner, as any movement can destroy the chance of success.

Trout also make a sipping sound when taking terrestrial flies which have been blown on to the water. The fishing technique is the same as for buzzers and emergers, but the flies of course are very different. If there is a good ripple, traditional palmered patterns may be used, and these may either be fished in the surface film or treated with floatant and fished dry. In calmer conditions, however, it pays to remove the palmer. Colour and size are important, although there is a fair amount of leeway in the overall dressing. Thus it is possible to use standard patterns such as the Bibio to represent hawthorn flies, and the Invicta to copy dung flies. It is also always worth having a Daddy-Long-Legs or Hopper at the ready, not just when the naturals are observed, but because these patterns seem to take fish on all sorts of occasions.

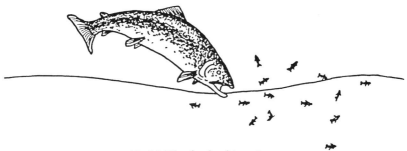

Fig 28 The fry-bashing rise

The Fry-Bashing Rise Fry are very important to the trout who will eagerly take the opportunity to put on valuable ounces for the long winter months ahead when food may be in short supply. The advantages of eating fry more than compensate for the energy expended in catching them. The charge through the shoals is usually an exciting and spectacular affair in which the trout make a high speed curving run, the bow-wave causing the fry to leap clear from the water like droplets in a fountain. The trout then return in a more leisurely manner to pick up the stunned victims.

Trout feeding on fry are very easy to locate, and most of the hot-spots will be common knowledge at any fishery lodge. At Chew we are very lucky to have the services of Bob Handford who is a keen fisherman with a great deal of local experience and knowledge. Like Bob, most fishery managers and staff will gladly help those who ask for advice.

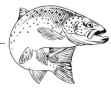

3

TECHNIQUE
AND TACTICS

WATERCRAFT

Whether fishing from boat or bank, it is always worth stopping for a while when arriving at the water, to consider the prevailing conditions and how any natural features may be used to advantage. Many fishermen make their way directly to well-known hot-spots, or to locations where they may have been successful on previous visits when the weather conditions were completely different. However, take account of all the available information: this not only allows full advantage to be taken of familiar fisheries, but enables skills to be acquired to tackle completely unknown waters when local advice may not be available.

BANK FISHING

The underwater contours may be assessed by studying the bank profile running down to the water's edge as it is often an approximate mirror image. Look for changes in contours such as ridges, creeks, streams or anything that might form a home to insect life or attract the curiosity of the passing trout. Special attention should be paid to bays and promontories since these are particularly efficient areas for channelling food. A wind blowing parallel to the bank will cause local increases in flow around a point, depositing large concentrations of food which will often lead to trout holding station in the areas of highest flow.

Once a fish-holding area has been located, a light-footed approach should be adopted, taking care not to advertise your presence. Thoughtless wading can destroy the fishing for others along a whole stretch of bank by sending the fish out into the middle of the lake. A trout's natural habitat is in the margins, and if it were not for the presence of man, these bankside areas would be teeming with fish right through the season — the first hour of any opening day always brings a very high catch rate for bank fishermen. Thus, if you are the first fisherman in an area, always start with your feet on terra firma.

The other common mistake is to start by casting too far — the repeated crashing

Careful wading in a flat calm at Wentwood

of the belly of a fly-line over the fish will send them scurrying away into open water. Cast only a few yards, gradually extending the cast along the bank as well as straight out, until the marginal areas have been fully exploited.

Bank vegetation such as bushes and trees will play host to a variety of species of terrestrials which are deposited on the water as the wind blows them towards the lake. It is particularly important to look for these areas in waters where there is limited sub-surface food, for the hungry trout will eagerly wait there for the wind-blown offerings.

Every water is at the mercy of the wind, but usually there is a prevailing wind direction which sets up feeding patterns and encourages the trout to patrol well-defined areas. Trout on the move and feeding near the surface normally travel upwind since this is their most efficient way of intercepting food. When their feeding run comes to an end because of a bank, for example, they will eventually move back downwind to their starting position quite quickly at depth. However, before doing this they may hold station for a while, particularly if the bank has a severe change in contour such as a bay or corner which holds a steady supply of food. Such hot-spots are usually crowded with anglers, but if the wind is blowing parallel to the bank, it may be possible to move downwind and intercept the fish in advance of the masses, casting out as far as possible across the wind with a team of imitative patterns. These should be fished statically, allowing the bow in the line to move the flies round in an arc, and above all remembering to tighten in the correct direction which keeps the tension in the line: this can sometimes mean striking in a direction contrary to your natural instincts.

Sometimes the fish will move past in a steady progression, whereas on other occasions they may remain in a shoal which might give five minutes of frantic activity followed by half an hour's wait. This shoaling can cause sudden panic in an attempt to cover the first fish as quickly as possible — the result is often a disastrous tangle which is not repaired until the fish have passed by. Thus, self-discipline and an unhurried approach are essential, as is the patience to hold station even when all goes quiet since the shoaling fish should eventually return.

The alert fisherman should always be on the look-out for wind (or calm) lanes. These are calm stretches of water, anything from a few feet to tens of yards in width, which form a natural trap for large amounts of food. Even on dour days the trout can be seen moving up these lanes, and on a good day the sport can be absolutely spectacular. On windy days, the water can be whipped up into a scum which lies on the calm lanes. This foam does not put the fish off at all, but seems to act as a protective umbrella giving them increased confidence, and it is not uncommon to see the dorsal and tail fins of large specimens as they mill around the scum lanes, oblivious to their vulnerability.

Noticing calm and scum lanes is second nature to the experienced boat fisherman, but it is not uncommon to find areas of bank from which they can be

A productive scum lane

reached. We have frequently seen such areas deserted, simply because they were remote from the recognised hot-spots, and have enjoyed some marvellous, uninterrupted fishing.

If there are no obvious signs of where to fish, a systematic approach is required: walk around the lake and make a couple of casts every few yards until that all-important tug is felt on the end of the line. Then there are two obvious tactics which may be employed.

The first tactic is used when there is no prior knowledge of stock-fish, and employs a team of nymphs since this should always tempt any fish (stockie or resident) which may be passing. A Stick Fly is perfect on the point, and a green tag can improve its effectiveness greatly, particularly if the water is coloured. A 'sedge' type pupa such as a green or amber nymph could go in the middle, with a drab-coloured buzzer on the top dropper. It is essential to fish these nymphs very slowly, and this is best achieved with a floating or intermediate line.

The second approach might be more effective if there is known to be a good head of recently stocked fish. Our favourite tactic would be to 'FTA' with a Viva on an intermediate line (see page 49), but leaving at least one imitative pattern such as a Stick Fly on a dropper.

BOAT FISHING

The boat fisherman can be just as perplexed when faced with a large expanse of water. Very often he will locate feeding fish by trial and error, motoring around the lake until he sees some underwater movement, or fishing in different areas until he feels that exciting pull.

Much of the watercraft already discussed still applies, but there may be additional hot-spots from 'false islands' in the middle of the lake. These can be seen at low water, either as a low island or by the appearance of weedy shallows which are usually given away by feeding swans. Needless to say, such areas can provide extremely productive contours and will quickly become apparent on your local waters; on visiting new waters their location should be a high priority — seek advice from the fishery staff, and procure a contour map of the lake from which they should be obvious.

Not only can swans help to locate productive shallow areas, they also stir up the weed with their long necks when feeding and release a lot of underwater nymphs. Fishing close to, or downwind of feeding swans, can therefore be a killing tactic and it is not only criminal, but also an uneducated and intolerant policy to curse them for being in the way and to try and scare them off.

James O. following in Dad's footsteps

Birds in general are, or should be, the fisherman's friend, adding to the overall quality of the environment and providing all sorts of tell-tale signs as to where the fish might be. Their top priority apart from survival is feeding, and in many cases they share the same food chain with the fish. The difference is, of course, that the birds can be identified half a mile away. Swooping swallows and swifts reveal hatching insects which must indicate an abundance of pupae (and hopefully trout) below the surface; grebes betray the presence of fry, and wherever there is an abundance of fry there should be a good concentration of brownies. But perhaps the most telling sign of all is to see gulls frantically descending on the water, as they pick up the maimed fry which have been attacked by trout in a feeding frenzy.

The boat fisherman has many advantages over his bank-fishing counterpart. Far more areas of the lake are accessible to him, which is particularly important in shallow reservoirs which have a lot of productive feeding grounds and false islands away from the bank, or extensive shallow contours. Those which have a large surface area for a given perimeter of bank also favour boats because the average distance of the fish from the bank is correspondingly large. All of these features make Chew Valley the perfect lake for the boat fisherman, whereas its sister reservoir Blagdon has a much greater bank area for its size, and the bank fishing is significantly improved. At the other extreme the water at Wimbleball shelves very steeply from the bank, and only a few yards out the depth can exceed the deepest parts of Chew. The most productive areas are usually about ten feet deep, and so the most effective tactic in this reservoir is also to explore the banks. Thus, whether to fish boat or bank should be decided by the nature of the lake.

Mobility is the other obvious advantage. A large reservoir from the bank can be a daunting prospect, and it can take a long time, and a lot of inconvenience, to move from one area to another, especially as this often involves getting back into the car, tackle and all. Moving position on the boats, however, is the easiest thing in the world, although the commonest mistake made by many fishermen is to anchor. Anchoring is generally a hit and miss affair: if you are over a shoal of fish, the chances are that you will catch a few very quickly and then spook the rest which will either move away or simply stop taking — it is far better to cover a hundred fish once each by drifting over them, than to cover the same fish a hundred times at anchor.

The worst offender is the selfish (or perhaps just ignorant) idiot who sees fish being caught by a drifting boat, and then anchors at the most productive point of the drift. This is not only extremely bad etiquette, but will probably ruin the fishing in what was previously a productive local area. It may be too much to hope that all of these hoodlums can be educated, but perhaps some fishery managers may one day take the lead by banning anchoring altogether except in emergencies.

Let us assume that in spite of trying the favourite drifts and having looked around the lake, you have had very little success and seen very few fish moving. This is different from knowing where the fish are, but failing to catch, in which case the solution lies in choosing the right pattern and applying it correctly. The answer is to use a systematic approach to explore the water until some feeding trout are located.

If the fish are not showing, they could be feeding near the bottom of the lake. If so, there is little chance of reaching fish which are in, say, forty feet of water unless the water clarity is exceptional, or unless you enjoy trolling cockerels behind the boat (which is a tactic that has no place in this book). The solution is therefore to keep to the productive areas of ten feet or so, where there is always a chance of bottom-feeding fish noticing the flies. Thus it is a good tactic to drift along a bank at a distance which depends on the contours, or to zig-zag along a shore drifting in towards the bank, bearing in mind at all times to keep a minimum distance of a hundred yards from any bank angler.

With two anglers in the boat, it is most effective to experiment with two different line densities. Unless conditions are so cold that the fish are known to be lying deep, which only really applies in early season, one angler should persevere with the floater and use a good percentage team which aims to cover most eventualities. The top fly should be a puller like a Soldier Palmer which can often

Two different styles on the edge of a calm lane

entice fish to the surface even though there may be nothing hatching. It is a good idea to have an imitative fly such as a Stick Fly, Buzzer or Pheasant Tail on the point, and on the middle dropper have a fly which is generally suggestive of life — try a flasher such as a Silver Invicta or Wickhams on a bright day, or a dull fly such as a Mallard and Claret or Connemara Black when it is overcast.

The other angler should try sinking lines. The intermediate may not get the flies down deep enough, and a Hi-Speed Hi-D can tend to pull the flies down too quickly. The perfect compromise is therefore the Wet-Cel 2. It is not a bad idea to put a Viva on the point since it can incite fish to attack it even when they have no intention of feeding. A suggestive fly like a Dunkeld is perfect for the middle dropper, and a buzzer can be an excellent imitative fly for the top dropper.

In sunk line fishing, the handling of the last stage of the retrieve is vital — anglers are often heard exclaiming how there was a great swirl at the end of the line as the flies were lifted off, and the ability to deal with this phenomenon is the major difference between a good and an indifferent sinking line fisherman. There is no way of knowing how many fish see our flies under the surface, but there is plenty of evidence to show that we get far more follows than takes. We must therefore always assume that a fish is following, and instead of lifting off suddenly, hold the flies in the water for a few seconds at the very least. A following fish will probably stay in watch for some time, and he may be tempted into making a mistake by moving the rod tip up and down a few times. This is simply FTA in another guise, but on hard days it can be the sole determining factor between success and failure. Furthermore, whereas FTA was previously applied to stock-fish, this tactic is a real killer for the wiser residential fish, particularly brownies.

The two most widely adopted methods of retrieving flies in front of a drifting boat are long-lining and short-lining. Long-lining was exploited to the full by the successful Bristol teams in the Benson and Hedges competitions, and although it is the less traditional technique, it has many advantages. Spotting a moving fish at long range and being able to cover it accurately means that if the cast is inaccurate, or if the fish is moving faster than expected or changes direction, then there is enough time for two or more casts at the same fish. Long-lining can be particularly effective on difficult days when the trout are either shy or reluctant to take the fly. Quite often they will be seen following in from a great distance, seemingly trying to make up their minds whether or not to take the offering. But if a fish has been intrigued for twenty yards it will quite often take the fly as it is dibbled in the surface before lift-off.

Long-lining does nonetheless have a few disadvantages. Quite often a fish will rise quite near to the boat just after a long line has been cast, necessitating a time-consuming line retrieve before it can be covered. In such situations the short-liner will obviously have the edge as he can lift off and cover the fish at once. Also, on days of particularly heavy wave the fish may be lying slightly deeper, and a short-line dibbling technique may be the more effective method. It is a wonderful sight to see an angler skilfully demonstrating short-line techniques, holding his team of flies interminably in the surface — he will seem to barely move the rod before lift-off, and yet this is when he frequently succeeds.

A great deal of co-operation is needed between the two boat partners, often referred to as 'observing the courtesies of the boat'. Technically two anglers fishing downwind have an angle of ninety degrees in which to cast, but for the sake of comfort, safety and practicability this arc should be reduced to about forty-five degrees on each side of the centre-line of the boat. This avoids any tangling of back-casts and in most situations permits more than enough water to be covered. Casting at right-angles to the boat should only be attempted after giving due warning.

Using all available angles can make the difference between success and failure. So often, anglers are seen casting consistently straight down-wind, and in a dour period this can become purely mechanical. In most circumstances trout will be travelling with their noses up-wind, so it is logical to cast across the waves as much as possible which will show the flies to more trout. It is also arguable that a fly appears more enticing when seen from a side angle than from behind.

Thus boat tactics are far more than a simple 'sit down and retrieve' affair, as there is so much that the angler can do to increase his chances of a trout. There is a huge variation in the speed, style and depth of retrieve, and attention to this is

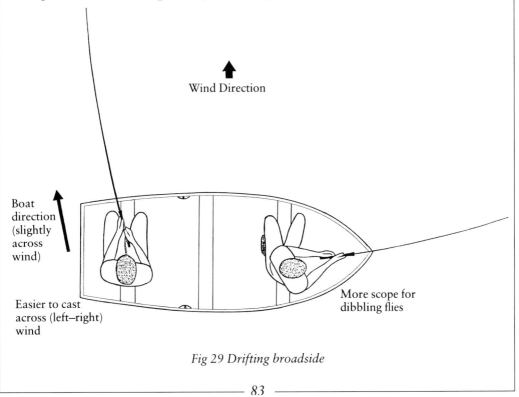

Fig 29 Drifting broadside

Netting behind the boat is easier without a drogue

probably the most important thing to bear in mind when conditions are hard. The action of a jerky or impatient retrieve is invariably transmitted down the line, and things can go from bad to worse (in both bank and boat fishing) unless a conscious effort is made to concentrate on getting it right. And practise looking for fish — in general terms, the more successful anglers will be those who can spot fish more readily, and this does not just mean seeing obvious rises when they occur, but includes recognising the more subtle signs of a trout's presence such as a flattening of the ripple or the merest innuendo. Good eye-sight enhanced by polaroid glasses is a pre-requisite which can rank just as highly as any aspect of tackle or technique.

The boat fisherman has to retrieve more quickly than his counterpart on the bank to allow for the forward motion of the boat. This requires a greater degree of skill in working the flies to represent the naturals, and it is therefore common practice to slow the boat down with a drogue. It does, however, have several disadvantages which should be considered before automatically using one (as is all too often the case). First, it causes many a lost fish as he dives beneath or round the boat. Second, it is an added inconvenience at the end of a drift, and can also lose precious seconds in having to be pulled in when moving across to intercept a shoal moving upwind. In practice, many anglers shrug their shoulders and miss a golden opportunity. And third, it is inconvenient when making fine adjustments to the position of the boat as is often necessary when drifting down a calm lane. Boats seldom drift parallel to the wind; on Chew, for example, there is a significant stern-first movement across the current. Finally when locating fish, it is an advantage to cover the water as quickly as possible. However, there are obviously other, more advantageous factors to be taken into account, and perhaps the most important is when using a sunk line, since even a slight reduction in boat speed can make that all important difference in letting the flies go down that little bit deeper.

As much as thoughtless anchoring and disturbance to bank anglers is bad etiquette, it is also extremely inconsiderate to motor across someone else's drift. A moving boat is generally accepted as putting fish down, and most boat fishermen seldom motor upwind over the drift they intend to fish next. On the other hand, we have observed that in fact a moving boat in open water (and it *must* be away from the bank) can actually induce fish to feed. On many occasions fish are either taken or seen immediately after stopping the boat, and it is important to take full advantage of this fact by casting out as quickly as possible at the start of a drift. This may simply be the trout's natural curiosity; it may also be that stock-fish, and the residents who wait underneath stock-fish cages for any pellets which escape the feeding frenzy, have learned to associate the arrival of a boat with food.

Conversely, under heavy angling pressure fish can all too soon learn of their dangers. This has been very evident over many years during the South-West Benson and Hedges heats on Wimbleball — on the final day of three hectic contests, when the trout in the clear water have been bombarded by all hosts of artificial patterns, they become noticeably boat shy and the best catches invariably come from the previously neglected areas. Fry feeders, too, can be put right off their feeding pattern by boats motoring over them.

THE LIGHT APPROACH

One of the rewards when preaching any kind of angling gospel is to see others gaining obvious success from following your recommendations. It is too easy to expound a theory which is only half-proven, or to describe a fly that happened to work well last week but does not have the benefit of any long-term testing. The most solid theories are often the most logical, and sound common sense in fishing has much to recommend it. For many seasons now, many experts have been extolling the virtues of lighter lines, lighter rods and finer tippets and, slowly, the 'fishing fine' theory has been gathering weight.

To many, fishing fine simply involves using a light leader, or at the very least a finer tippet. Whilst this is undoubtedly effective, it is by no means the whole story, and the concept in fact involves a more delicate, subtle and refined approach to every aspect of fly fishing on stillwater. It means forsaking those 9- and 10-weight shooting heads, and moving away from poker-stiff carbon rods to something very much lighter and forgiving. Above all, it involves thinking about why such moves are successful, why they lead to improved catch rates, and why they give us so much more satisfaction than the coarser, heavyweight tackle.

Line weight should be the first consideration. The AFTMA scale is now adopted across the world, and classifies line weights from 1 to 12. With the broadest possible categorisation, lines from 2 to 6 are the province of the river and stream man, 6 to 10 are for stillwaters, and 8 to 12 cover the spectrum of salmon fishing. However, it is just these categories which have blinkered anglers for so long. Stillwater fly fishermen have generally shied away from anything less than AFTMA 7, thinking that it would not give them the kind of distance casting they wanted. With the new carbon rods, however, line weights of 4, 5 and 6 can be cast comfortably twenty-five yards with a balanced outfit. Probably of more significance is the fact that a light line can carry out a team of flies or even heavily weighted nymphs, and here we come back to balance: provided it is used with the appropriate rod, there is no reason why a 4- or 5-weight line will not perform such a task perfectly.

The most tangible benefit of the lighter line is the drastic reduction in disturbance on the water surface. Obviously the splash made by an 8-weight, as compared to a 5-, must seem to the fish like a plank landing on the surface. Whether fishing from boat or bank, the principle is identical: the less disturbance the line makes, the less the chance of spooking the fish, and the greater the chance of catching him. This is never more true than in conditions of flat calm when even the slightest surface disturbance is magnified many times, and particularly in evening rises which often occur as the surface flattens.

The final section of nylon between the fly-line and the fly is the section of tackle which is most crucial in deceiving the fish. General tackle and fly selection is important, but if you get the leader diameter wrong, the fish will see it and turn away — on those occasions when fish are feeding all around with abandon yet steadfastly ignoring your offering, this could be the reason and the time has come to start fishing fine.

On our home waters of Chew and Blagdon there are many established experts who will never go below 7lb breaking strain for their leaders, and quite often they are highly successful. However, in conditions of near or flat calm their lack of success is highly conspicuous, whereas those who have taken a drop in leader diameter will be catching fish. We hardly ever fish heavier than 6lb double strength and will frequently go well below this, not because of misplaced purism, but simply because we have proved to ourselves that catch rates can be vastly increased by this one simple expedient. With a soft rod and braided leader, dry sedge or spent midge can be fished on 3lb leaders with total confidence. CO sometimes even fishes 2½lb double strength leaders from the boat with a team of small traditional flies.

Steve Pope – master of the flat calm

A certain amount of practice will be a good thing, as it takes a little time to get used to a lighter leader. Gentle striking is necessary, though the soft rod and braided leader will, of course, cushion the strike and allow more than a few liberties to be taken.

Such is theory. Fishing fine will undoubtedly improve your catches and is a sound and solid avenue to better fishing. But even beyond that, it will improve your enjoyment of fishing by creating a greater challenge and sense of achievement. Finer tippets will result in more fish seeing your fly rather than your line, and will therefore result in more takes and ultimately more fish in the bag. And the warm, inner glow that comes from successfully using such tactics can only be experienced.

DRY FLY

Five years ago, the use of dry fly on stillwater was regarded as a minor tactic. A mere handful of anglers were prepared to use it, and even then it would usually be reserved for flat calms when nothing else was working. It was a kind of last resort: few people had ever tried it, and even fewer had any real confidence in it — it was even regarded as rather eccentric, and its exponents treated with some derision.

How things have changed! There has been a tremendous upsurge in the use of the dry fly, and it should be said that much of this popularity is due to competition anglers, since it is through them that the effectiveness of the method has become known and the current level of interest created.

Some myths should at once be dispelled: dry fly tactics can be employed on stillwater at any time and in any water conditions. Their use is not restricted to calm conditions, nor are they evening-only tactics. Indeed, dry flies left on the surface in a big mid-day heatwave can pull fish from nowhere, when there is no sign on the surface of any activity. This is probably because on most stillwaters, and particularly those with sparse sub-surface fly life, fish will often be cruising at depths of several feet, depending on water clarity, looking for food but without advertising their presence.

We have been convinced about the value of the dry fly for many years. The use of a tiny dry sedge has tempted many a resident brownie from weedy corners of Blagdon when other tactics have failed. In fact, the finest definition of fly fishing is this: a lone angler, stalking the banks of one of the oldest reservoirs in the country, spotting individual rising fish that are totally selective in their feeding on adult sedge, and casting a size 14 dry fly on a 3lb tippet. In weed-covered areas of Blagdon this is a challenge indeed, and the angler has done well if he manages to land one in three fish hooked.

Recently, dry fly has really come to the fore in boat fishing, and is undoubtedly the method most in vogue at the moment. Some tremendous bags of trout have been caught, not just in number but also in size. It is, however, too easy to become too preoccupied with the method, as is evident by the erratic catch rates of many of the dry fly specialists. As in every angling situation, watercraft is needed to read the conditions correctly and assess the viability of the technique on any given day.

Dry fly will often entice the better quality resident fish which are immune to the normal sub-surface offerings, and attention must therefore be paid to presentation and minimising leader diameter — such fine diameter line requires a careful design of leader to prevent the fly and nylon falling in a heap on the water. The leader must not be greased or it will stand out like hawser on the surface of the water; in fact, use 'mud' to remove the shine and assist the leader to penetrate the surface film where it is less visible. Some would argue that it is more important to submerge the nylon than to fish fine; we would advocate *both* precautions.

Dry fly fishing falls conveniently into two categories, namely dry and semi-dry: the flies are different, and so too are the ways in which they are fished.

The Flies There are three basic styles of dry fly that we use: emergers, hoppers and shipman style buzzers. In very general terms emergers are used to best effect at the beginning of a rise and Shipman buzzers will perform during an established rise or, at least, when there are plenty of visible moving fish. The hopper is more of a fly for all occasions. It has a more general appeal and in this respect it could be termed as more of a suggestive than imitative dry fly. Indeed, it is so effective that on any day that appears to be 'right' for dry fly we would think very hard before removing the hopper from the cast.

There are, of course, other specialised patterns which we use when a closer match to hatch is required (for example, sedge fishing in early evening) but in 90 per cent of circumstances these three basics will suffice.

Modern Dry Fly This is all about fishing a fly right on the surface, and when clearly identified naturals are on the water, this presents few problems. A Mayfly in the spring or a Daddy in September are simple cases of straight copy, and these have always been considered essentials in a fly box. Less commonly used,

'Catch and release' with the dry fly

however, are adult buzzers and sedges — in the past, recognised authorities actually stated that the stillwater trout rarely, if ever, took the adult insects. Yet it is now known that these form a major part of the trout's diet, and today the patterns are well established and relatively easy to tie.

Less obvious are the dry flies which qualify as suggestive patterns. Just as the Pheasant Tail or Stick Fly are suggestive of natural sub-surface food items rather than close copies, so too are many dry flies. They seek to give an overall shape, outline or silhouette which will suggest a rough copy of perhaps several natural insects, and as such they have proved highly effective. Whereas the traditional dry flies were tied to be a perfect imitation, many modern patterns pay little attention to the detail on the top of the fly body since it is invisible to the trout. In fact, they take advantage of this fact by adding white feathers, wool or wings to help the angler focus his attention on the pattern at long range. This is particularly useful in a good ripple when even a large fly can be difficult to spot at a distance.

Visibility is of crucial importance and this applies not only to the trout but also to the angler. A small 'false wing' is useful especially if white hackle fibre is used as it helps the angler to see the fly even in fairly heavy water. This little wing is also an integral part of some emerger patterns as it helps to form the silhouette on the water surface.

Colour is also greatly signficant as the trout can be extremely selective. Obviously you should match the imitation as closely as possible to the hatching natural. This has particular relevance when, for example, Hawthorn or Dungfly are appearing or in other local terrestrials of a pronounced colour. Strangely enough, it seems that colour could be important even when there is no case for close copy: we have had huge successes with a medium claret emerger when the only fly life in evidence has been an olive buzzer. Such is the fickle nature of trout and the uncertainty of fly fishing.

General suggestive dry fly patterns are fairly uncomplicated patterns, yet few are available over the counter — perhaps the concept is still too new. They are, therefore, strictly for the angler who ties his own, and focus strongly on outline, often with judicious use of seal's fur. The fur is usually picked out quite liberally with a dubbing needle or velcro pad to keep the fly clear of the surface film.

Two crucial points need to be made, and the first concerns the use of floatant. Many anglers apply Permafloat or Gink too late, often at the last minute before fishing; in fact the best way is to treat the flies at the tying bench so they have a chance to dry out thoroughly, and the floatant can then really penetrate the body and fibres of the fly — an additional application before use will make the fly very buoyant indeed. Permafloat is straightforward to apply, but Gink is a much more viscous floating agent which needs to be applied thoroughly but sparingly. Because of its consistency, it is easy to apply too much at first, clogging the hackles of the fly. The trick is to warm a small amount between the fingers which thins it and makes it easier to work into the fibres; this is particularly relevant in cold weather when Gink can be extremely viscous. Any fly treated thus will rest on the surface film extremely well; but if Gink is worked into buoyant materials like elk or deer hair, the fly will be almost impossible to sink.

The second point concerns the gauge of hook wire: despite the temptation to use heavier hooks for big stillwater trout, it is imperative to stick to lighter wires — all the floatant in the world is no match for a heavyweight hook which will quickly cut through the surface film. Lighter gauge, high quality wire hooks are perfectly adequate for dry fly since there is usually more control over the strike. Most of our tying is done on Kamasan B400, B405 or B170 hooks — there is no need to look further.

As a generalisation the hopper is best tied on B400 as is the Shipman buzzer. However, emergers and, to some extent, smaller hopper sizes, should be tied on the slightly heavier Kamasan B170s. This enables the body of the fly to sit in the surface film and gives a far better profile in the trout's window.

When it comes to actually fishing these flies, there is a good deal of latitude in the technique. The static retrieve is the most common, which from a drifting boat really means casting out and only retrieving enough line to ensure there is no slack, with the fly essentially motionless. In most conditions this is a good method, but in flat calms it is absolutely essential. It is probably most effective when casting at specific fish; if you spot a moving fish and can predict his direction of travel from the rise-form, give him plenty of 'forward lead': this means dropping the fly a couple of yards from his last known position, where he is most likely to see it.

Another school of thought advocates moving the dry fly on the surface, sometimes creating a considerable wake. This is not unlike dibbling a bob fly in the surface, but has the advantage of being practical at long range. It obviously works best in rougher conditions, but in our experience is best used in conjunction with the static technique. Quite often, when a trout is being fussy and swirling around the static fly without taking, a sudden gentle movement from a figure-of-eight retrieve can induce him into a positive take.

When fish are being particularly fussy it pays to give extra special attention to both presentation and leader treatment. Obviously, clean turnover of the leader is needed and we find that it helps to control the last few yards of the cast with the left hand. This premature 'stopping' of the cast gives vastly improved turnover.

You should frequently treat the leader with a sinking compound: if it lies on the surface than all other aspects of presentation will be lost. Similarly, it is imperative that you keep in direct touch with the flies at all times. This is particularly relevant in a fast drifting boat and care should be taken to take up the slack yet, at the same time, not to move the flies. The best lightening reactions on the strike are totally negated by a slack line.

Semi-Dry Techniques Most of the real development is taking place in semi-dry fly fishing, to the extent where it is almost a genuinely original method. Very simply, it involves fishing the fly in, rather than on, the water surface, and there are two reasons why this method is so effective. First, a lot of natural insects become trapped in the surface film, particularly in calm conditions, both aquatic species such as buzzers and sedges which rise from the lake bed, and terrestrials that get blown onto the water where they struggle and drown. Thus a conventional dry fly, sitting on the surface on its well-treated hackles, will not be imitating such food.

The second reason is that a fly resting *on* the surface can only be seen if it appears in the trout's window, and it should be remembered that this corresponds roughly to twice the depth of the trout. However, any submerged parts of a fly are visible both inside and outside the window.

The situation is tailor-made for emergers: these have been used on rivers for many years and represent the insect at the point of hatching from pupa to adult. This process can take some time, particularly in calm conditions, and often results in the fish gorging themselves in the surface film. Semi-dry imitation also includes the spent flies such as midges that fall onto the surface to die.

As with the fully dry flies, these patterns need to be tied on lightweight hooks with the application of floatant. However, it is important that only the front part of the fly is treated, the hackle for instance, so that the body will submerge — the body can be helped to sink, in fact, by the use of sinkants such as Zink.

Finally, there is a very effective hybrid technique which uses a lightweight nymph on the middle dropper suspended between two static dry flies. Our own favourite pattern on the Bristol reservoirs is a Claret Buzzer tied on a size 12 Kamasan B400; the best of both worlds is obtained, and it is fascinating to see how on any given day the majority of the takes will come to either one method or the other. This just shows how important it is to have a flexible approach in fishing, to be willing to change tactics when the need arises. With this particular hybrid technique, all concentration is naturally centred on the visible dry flies, and it can be quite a surprise when the rod is suddenly pulled from your hand as a fish takes the nymph.

When To Use Dry Fly Techniques Sometimes it is obvious when to use dry fly since you can watch the naturals on the water being taken. Even then, however, it is amazing how many stillwater fishermen see this happening and yet persist with nymphs or something even less appropriate. There is still a great deal of natural reluctance about dry fly fishing, but at times it can mean the difference between a blank day and an eight-fish limit in half-an-hour.

The very general rule on the strike is to wait for about one second and then lift into the fish in one slow, but positive, movement. Fish will normally turn down on the fly and an overly fast reaction will either result in a lip hook or no hook hold at all. The only exception to this is when you see the trout's neb or when you hear the positive sound of a sipping rise: in both these instances the strike should be immediate.

If fish are continually swirling but not taking then you should either change the fly or reduce the diameter of the leader. It may also mean that further leader treatment is required with sinking compound but, more probably, that the leader is too heavy for the prevailing conditions. As a rule of thumb we all favour 6lb double strength for 80 per cent of our fishing.

The use of floatant is an art in itself. We always apply Gink as a fairly light dressing at the tying bench. Shipman buzzers should receive an all-over coating whereas with emergers and hoppers it is best only to Gink the thorax. This results in a far better attitude of the fly on the water.

On some occasions, rise-forms can give some clue as to the trout's diet of dry flies; but one of the most obvious, and yet overlooked, comes from spooning. The stomach contents in a spoon are usually closely mashed together and the details not always easily visible; all too often a diet of brown buzzers, for example, is inferred from the spoon — but if the contents are placed in a jar of water and examined closely, structures like legs and wings might be noticed. Need we say more?

One of the glorious things about dry fly is that the fish do not need to be showing on the surface for the method to be effective. This is particularly true in clear water or on days when there is a combination of calm weather and clear water. On one particularly memorable day at Wimbleball we were pulling fish from depths of ten feet or more with very small black hoppers. The fish were taking with supreme confidence even on a day when the favourite tactic was a slow retrieve on intermediate line. There are times when very little is showing, and even less is being caught; under such conditions, when there is very little food in the water, trout tend to look up to the surface for food. On several occasions, when there hasn't been a single take to sub-surface techniques, we have been able to rise fish at the rate of a dozen an hour by the use of a static dry fly. This is a favourite technique at Grafham, and we have often experienced it on Chew and other lakes so it must be a generally applicable method. Such sport can be supremely exciting, as takes come from nowhere; sometimes it is a crash, at others the merest sip which will be missed if you blink. Again, visibility in the fly pattern, and the greatest concentration on the part of the angler, are needed.

SUNK LINE NYMPHING

Nymph fishing is nearly always associated with the floating line because it allows the flies to be moved very slowly to imitate the natural, and the range of depths can be varied depending on factors such as the weight of the fly and length of the leader. A slow movement cannot easily be achieved with a sinking line which tends to pull the flies downwards in an unrealistic arc.

However, if slow sinkers or intermediates are used, the line may sink at a comparable rate to the fly and therefore still allow a natural movement. With the submerged line there is no need for a long leader, and as the fly no longer hangs vertically below the end of the line, takes tend to register much more positively. This should be the first choice, therefore, when the fish are holding a few feet down. It can also be of great benefit in a big wave, because a floater will ride the waves and consequently have a lot of slack between the fly and angler. It is common indeed to hear of fish not taking the fly properly in such conditions, but it is not the trout but the tackle which is to blame. In very rough conditions, an intermediate, or even a Wet-Cel 2, will cut through the waves and allow the angler to keep in direct contact with the flies.

With fast sinking lines it becomes much more difficult to move flies in anything like a natural manner, but there is one tactic which can be used from a boat or a steeply sloping bank. It came to our notice when we observed that buzzers fished on the sinker would eight times out of ten take trout on the lift at the end of a sunk line retrieve.

It is very temping to think of buzzer feeding taking place exclusively near the surface, but any rise must start from the bottom of the lake. The pupae are vulnerable the moment they leave the shelter of the mud and weeds, and the trout intercept them all the way up to the surface. Buzzers moving vertically upwards on the sinker are a good representation of these ascending pupae, and it should therefore come as no surprise that such a large proportion of trout are taken on the final lift. Floating line fishermen will often catch the first trout on the point fly during the early stages of a rise, and this is simply an indication of the trout moving up in the water with the main concentration of food.

Fishing the sinking line obviously comes into its own when there is little or no surface activity, and when floating line tactics, including the dry fly, have failed to raise fish. Under these conditions the fish are very often not looking to the surface because there is an abundance of food down below — even if they are not feeding at the lower levels, any fly which they recognise as food may trigger a response. It is a matter of going through the sink rates from, say, an intermediate to a Hi-Speed Hi-D, and having the patience to persevere until the holding depth is located.

The common tendency to fish the sinking line fast must be avoided. Remember that you are aiming to imitate the slow upwards movement of the natural, and that this is best carried out in smooth, slow draws with a pause now and then, to represent the pupa on its halting ascent to the surface. Think how the natural moves in the water to prevent you moving the artificials too quickly or jerkily. At the end of the retrieve, when the top dropper reaches the surface, hold the flies in the water for at least a few seconds, for quite often a hesitant fish may be following which will eventually take as the fly hangs motionless.

In tying the artificial, bear in mind that the light intensity a few feet down in many of our stillwaters is reduced by the coloured water. It therefore does no harm to make the buzzers easily visible on size 10 hooks with slightly exaggerated

Buzzers on the lift

white breather tubes, but remember to keep the bodies reasonably slim to maintain the correct slender profile. The colour is not especially important, though it is sensible to imitate the natural as closely as possible. We have had a lot of success with claret, black, brown and green, and two or three different colours can be fished on the same cast.

The method can be particularly effective for taking brown trout, which can sometimes be very difficult to catch during a rise due to the way they move in the water. Rainbows will usually hold a fairly shallow depth and be clearly visible as they move in search of surface food, so it is relatively straightforward to judge their direction, and to estimate where to cast to intercept them. Brownies, on the other hand, have an annoying habit of holding at a depth of several feet, coming straight up in the water to take the fly, and then moving immediately back down again. With a sinker, the fly spends more of its time at the trout's holding level and judging by the success rate, this can sometimes be a great advantage, even during a rise!

MISMATCHING THE HATCH

The following conditions have occurred on Chew and many other reservoirs during just about every season we can remember, usually when there is an absence of reasonably sized pupae combined with an abundance of tiny fly life on the surface. The trout become totally pre-occupied with mopping up these tiny insects off the surface, and remain very high in the water, moving upwind with random zig-zag motions as flies come into view. This behaviour is most evident from the boats, when it is often possible to spend most of the day covering fish on nearly every cast. The numbers of visible fish can be staggering, and yet there are usually a lot of rather empty-looking bass bags at the end of the day and some baffled and beaten fishermen.

Why are trout so difficult to catch under these conditions? It is a common misconception that a very small fly is required. Although most of the naturals correspond to a size 20 or smaller, we seldom go below a size 14 and usually use the 10 to 12 range. The fundamental problem is not the difficulty of imitating tiny naturals, it is getting the trout to actually see the artificial.

In terms of the trout's view of the surface, light entering the water is refracted (or bent) downwards as shown in the diagram, with no light being able to reach the trout at an angle greater than about 48 degrees. The surface therefore appears as a circular 'window' of light, with a diameter roughly equal to twice the depth of the fish in the water, and this window is surrounded by an opaque 'mirror' through which no light can reach the trout directly from above the surface. As a result, dry flies which rest *on*, rather than *in*, the surface film are invisible to the trout unless they lie within its window.

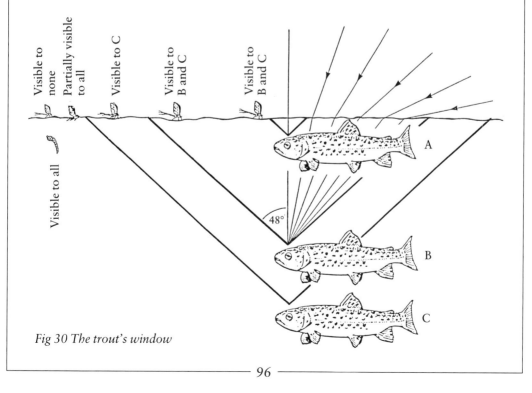

Fig 30 The trout's window

Two ways of keeping out of the trout's window

Why these surface-feeding fish are so difficult to catch should now be apparent. If we assume that they cruise a couple of inches below the surface, their entire field of view of surface flies is a mere four inches. Covering one of these fish therefore requires pin-point accuracy, but even a successful cast carries a risk because the sudden arrival of the fly so close to the fish may put it down.

Of course, semi-dry flies will be visible outside the window, and so will wet flies as long as they are no deeper than the couple of inches assumed for the upward-looking trout. However, with the trout's feeding instincts in this case concentrated in the surface window, any partially or fully submerged fly will have to make its presence felt to attract his attention. It is this ingredient in a fly which forms the basis of many of the successful patterns.

The trick is to catch the trout off balance, distract him from his mopping up by drawing his attention away from his tiny surface window, and induce him to take before he realises what has happened.

A bushy fly such as a Muddler will alert the trout's attention by remaining high in the water and creating a disturbance on the surface. Alternatively, a very bright fly — the red end of the spectrum seems to be most effective for surface fishing — can often catch the trout's eye. The Peach Doll, and by 'peach' we mean the brightest fluorescent orange available, works extremely well, and so does the Grenadier since it is both bright and bushy yet still imitates the natural. The original V1 (an abbreviation for Grenadier Variant Number One) was invented as one of a range of very bright Grenadier patterns for use under these conditions.

Sometimes with these non-imitative methods, it is inadvisable to give the trout too long to think about the distraction since he will soon realise his mistake and turn away; thus the fish which follow the fly tend to take almost at once or not at all. It therefore pays to retrieve quickly, and this has the added advantage of keeping the flies high in the water and increasing their wake. In such circumstances, the flies can be lifted off the surface after a couple of seconds in the hope that the sudden acceleration will provoke the fish to take before he has had a chance to think about his mistake. If this fails, there is nothing to lose by covering the fish again, since the sudden reappearance of a lost fly can sometimes trigger a last ditch response.

Finally, we would hate to leave you with the impression that deceiving these surface feeders is easy; even the very best fishermen have difficulty, and those catching limits may have covered hundreds of fish in the process.

4

FLY-TYING

Although it is possible to catch plenty of fish on commercially tied flies, such patterns will always be based on someone else's interpretation. This is quite acceptable for the traditional patterns which have stood the test of time, providing they are tied correctly with high quality hooks and materials. In fact, the tying of some traditionals with difficult winging materials can be rather time-consuming, so quite a few expert fishermen buy their standard patterns off the shelf. This relies on a thorough knowledge of tying techniques and of the flies themselves to be able to judge whether the commercial pattern is up to standard — all too often these flies are tied on totally inappropriate wire gauges.

Beginners obviously have to rely on commercial (or other people's) flies, but with more experience the thinking fisherman will want to incorporate some of his own observations and ideas into patterns. If his subsequent interpretation is correct the fly will obviously be more effective, but he will have no way of knowing, even if he is mistaken, unless he can actually tie the pattern and experiment with it. The inability to do this will inevitably lead to a lot of frustration, resulting in loss of confidence and subsequently reduced catch rates. Thus, mastering fly-tying techniques will improve catch rates significantly, although this does not require the skills necessary to win prizes: it means developing the understanding of those features of a fly which are necessary to deceive the trout.

Fly-tying is not explained in detail here: there are already many good books available, and the angling press often publishes articles which cover the subject admirably. Furthermore none of our flies would win prizes in fly-dressing competitions, although we would also argue that such perfection is unnecessary for our purposes. We prefer to place the emphasis on the trout's, rather than the human admirer's, reaction to the fly.

THE BASIC APPROACH

Flies should be tied to suggest life, and the incorporation of some form of movement can often be a great advantage. Realism, however, demands other considerations. There is a parallel here with some of the French Impressionist paintings which can catch the eye more effectively with their imprecise brushstrokes than many of the more detailed pictures, and still convey the scene perfectly. Similarly traditional flies give an immediate impression of a food-form, even though their detail does not necessarily coincide closely with the natural. In fact, their general nature can suggest a whole variety of food forms, and this can be a great advantage when the trout's feeding pattern is uncertain.

In rough water, attention to detail is relatively unimportant, and features such as hackles or wings which disturb the water and bring the fly to life can be far more effective than a perfect copy of the natural. In calm water, however, when the trout has plenty of time for inspection, attention to detail can be essential.

Before designing a pattern, it is important to think carefully about its intended use. Flies can be loosely defined as 'Pullers', 'Suggesters' or 'Imitators'. A Puller's prime purpose is to attract (or distract) the trout, without necessarily resembling any natural species. It can do this either by water disturbance (as in Soldier Palmers, Muddlers) which is most effective in rough conditions, or by colour (Peach Dolls) which is ideal for coloured water. It is also important to decide whether the fly will be fished high in the water. If so, it may be best to include hackles to create a surface wake, whereas a highly mobile wing such as marabou may be more effective below the surface. The latter, in fact, corresponds to what is normally regarded as a lure, though it is no more a lure than many heavily palmered conventional patterns.

Imitators are obviously flies and nymphs which are tied to resemble the natural as closely as possible. Some lures also fall into this category since they are good representations of fry — from the purist's point of view a lure such as an Appetiser ought to be far more acceptable than many traditional patterns which resemble nothing in particular, though they would be horrified at the thought.

Suggesters cover many traditional winged flies and the more striking nymph patterns. They are a compromise between natural appearance and attraction, and are a good bet on days when the trout's feeding habits are uncertain. A Silver Invicta, for example, can represent a small fry or a hatching sedge, but it can also work in a buzzer rise and has an attracting flash in bright conditions.

CHOICE OF MATERIALS

Hooks For many years the best hooks were handmade by craftsmen; the first machine-made ones were cheaper but inferior which held true until a few years ago — now, however, the best hooks are machine-made and, regrettably for British industry, are manufactured in Japan. What gives the Japanese hooks the edge is stronger, higher carbon content steel, and incredibly sharp chemically etched points which improve hooking qualities substantially.

Even when restricting the choice of hooks to Kamasan and Drennan, there is still a vast range to choose from. Some patterns are so close that there is obviously room for personal preference, but the hooks mentioned here provide a comprehensive selection which is sufficient for most needs.

For dry fly and top of the water nymph fishing, the Kamasan B400 in sizes 10 and 12 is the panacea. For smaller flies, the size 14 is rather too fine for reservoir trout, and the shorter shank B170 is preferable in a size 12.

The B400 and B170 hooks are extremely light yet surprisingly strong, but when using such fine wire there will always be the odd fish which will cause the hook to straighten. Indeed, certain hook-holds against bone can cause some quite heavy wire hooks to open out. Therefore, when fishing close to the surface film is less important, it is advisable to use heavier wire — this also helps the fly reach its fishing depth. The ideal, all-round reservoir hook is the Drennan Wet-Fly Supreme.

Some nymphs need to be dressed on a longer shank hook, such as the Drennan Carbon Nymph and the Kamasan B830. The latter is especially good for our all-time favourite Stick Fly, whilst the slightly longer shank of the Drennan Carbon Nymph is perfect for Damsels.

Quite often, a fast sinking fly is needed, and since artificial weighting is banned by international rules, the choice of a heavy wire hook is of paramount importance. The Kamasan B175 will keep a fly reasonably submerged in a good wave, but to get the fly right down, use the Drennan Traditional Wet and the Kamasan B160. It is not uncommon to be accused of fishing leaded flies when using these hooks, which make quite a 'plop' on hitting the water.

Hackles A genetic cock cape — one produced specifically for its feathers — can cost a small fortune and in fact merely enables the nymph and wet fly fisherman to catch fewer fish. The long-held belief has been that stiff hackles are better for dry flies since they ride higher on the surface film, but many dry patterns are actually far more effective when partially submerged, and the very successful dry buzzers have no hackle at all. Overall, our view is that stiff hackles are a disadvantage for some dry flies, and a downright handicap for wet patterns.

In fishing a submerged fly, the hackles are required to move to give the suggestion of life. Hen feathers give far more movement than cock hackles, and (English) partridge brown back or grey neck feathers increase the movement even further. However, a very soft hackle will sometimes hug the body of a fly without moving out again; this problem can be overcome to some extent by winding the hackle very close to the front of the body or immediately in front of a stiffer cock hackle. Thus, the base of the feather is forced to stand out at right angles to the hook, and this helps the hackle to kick back again.

Tying a soft hackle 'with a kick' does give a rather specialised profile. The most general solution is to choose a hackle which is soft enough to give adequate movement, but just stiff enough to move back from the body. The most suitable compromise is best described as a soft cock, as found in many of the (larger) Chinese capes, or a stiff hen. In rough conditions, slightly stiffer hackles are more useful as they attract the trout by disturbing the water more, though they should not be so stiff as to give no movement.

Of the variety of capes on the market, the basic light red game is usually a good, all-round compromise since it has a natural appearance which is unlikely to arouse any alarm signals. Lighter hackles, such as honey, can show up better against a darker body, and a similar contrasting effect which may enhance visibility can be obtained from badger or Greenwells capes. Dyed capes are, of course, available for various specific patterns.

There are also some capes for special effects, of which the jungle cock is perhaps the best known. The import of jungle cock capes is illegal, but birds are bred specially in this country. Feathers of a specified size can now be bought loose, and this is by far the most cost-effective method of obtaining them, providing you are willing to forgo the status symbol which seems to be associated with possessing a full cape. Jungle cock eyes are expensive, but can greatly enhance some patterns, giving an impression of breather filaments or wing cases for example, but perhaps more importantly they provide a degree of contrast in a fly which can significantly enhance its effectiveness. In spite of many attempts at imitation, both man-made and by using alternative feathers, there seems to be no satisfactory substitute.

When using jungle cock eyes in a fly, it is better to make the eyes slightly too small than too big, otherwise the end result can appear rather unnatural. Also, while it is more fashionable to own a cape from a mature bird in which the eyes have a beautiful orange colouration, the whiter eyes seem to catch more fish!

Body Materials Most natural bodies are fairly neat affairs, but smooth silk manufactured ones just do not seem to convey the all-important ingredient of life, and the concept of impressionism is therefore of particular importance. The adult body of the orange silver midge exemplifies the problems of exact imitation: it appears to be a bright orange, but close inspection reveals that it actually consists of crimson and grey bands — any artificial which tries to copy these bands cannot hope to convey the overall impression of orange, whereas the ragged orange seal's fur on a Grenadier works extremely well.

Seal's fur has a natural translucence which is increased by teasing out the fibres slightly. Further suggestion of life can be obtained by mixing different colours and by using a rib in the tying. The mixing of furs is best achieved in a coffee blender, with a round cardboard sheet placed just above the blade to keep the seal's fur in the right place. Do *not*, however, hold the cardboard down with fingers! Phosphor Yellow can really enliven a fly when mixed with other colours (as illustrated on page 109), though the effect is so startling that its main use is as a puller.

One way of bringing seal's fur really to life is to tie it very sparsely over a silk underbody — red is a good colour, but gold or silver tinsels can also be used, and the potential for experimentation is enormous.

Buzzers often have a translucent drab brown appearance. We have experimented with polythene over brown silk bodies, but without any great success. Brown seal's fur works well, but arguably the best material is the fur from the root of a hare's ear. This is a dark greyish-brown colour with several light strands, and it sticks out from the body in a way which suggests life without really imitating anything exactly — another classic example of impressionism. Using this material for buzzers simply extends the principle used in the well-known Gold-Ribbed Hare's Ear, a fly generally accepted as representing a hatching olive and another example of the rib being vital to the overall pattern.

The small fibres in many herls can produce good natural imitations with plenty of small-scale movement. Peacock herl is the most useful all-rounder, and can add life to a fly in addition to, or instead of, hackles; its drab nature is so natural that it will catch fish in most circumstances. In a flat calm, the small amount of movement is far more natural than the larger scale motion of a hackle, and in these circumstances flies such as the Diawl Bach and Stick Fly are particularly effective. This herl seems to be much more effective when it is submerged slightly, so it is better to use Hare's Ear as an alternative for fishing close to the surface film.

Finally, there is the use of gold, silver or several other tinsels for fly bodies. These obviously have their advantages for imitating fry, but it is amazing how closely the gold-bodied Dunkeld can resemble a buzzer in the water. Flashers have an attracting property all of their own which not surprisingly tends to be more effective on bright days. However, silver flies in particular can vary quite unpredictably from being deadly to hopeless, so their use involves a considerable amount of trial and error.

Wings Wings serve a multitude of purposes on a wet trout fly, but ironically their primary purpose is seldom to imitate the wings of an insect. Below the water surface there is only limited winged insect life, so for a traditional pattern to represent a real winged fly, it needs to be fished high in the water. A good example would be the use of an Invicta to imitate a hatching sedge, or a Greenwells during a hatch of olives.

Hen pheasant wings on the Silver Invicta are a good representation of the back of a small fry and are the perfect complement to its silver body. The barred bronze colouration in the mallard wings (body) of a Dunkeld, and the white cheeks (wing cases), can give a marvellous representation of a buzzer when submerged. In both these flies, the contrasting dark wing provides a much more realistic impression to the rather flashy body, irrespective of imitating any specific species, and the effectiveness is seriously impaired if the wing is lost. In our experience, even a Wingless Wickhams is made more effective by using a medium to dark red game hackle, emphasising how important contrast can be. Some wings, in particular the black and white barred teal or wood duck feathers, provide an enticing contrast in their own right.

The other important property of wings is their mobility. Bronze mallard (or the dyed grey mallard substitute) and hen pheasant centre tails are both soft enough to have this advantage in addition to their natural appearance, and can be used as the basis for any wet fly collection. Teal gives a similar effect, and has even greater properties of attraction; blue mallard and the much neglected green teal have somewhat less movement, but their irridescent properties (common to many beetles, for example) can sometimes more than compensate for this.

If movement is a prime requisite in a winged fly, and accepting that there is no point in actually trying to represent a wing, then marabou is a very useful material. No one ever doubts its effectiveness on lures such as the Viva and Appetiser, but surprisingly it is rarely used on traditional wet flies.

Tails Most underwater fly life has at most three tail filaments, and if exact imitation is the priority, then very few patterns qualify. But like the wings, an impressionistic tail can add far more to a fly than would a simple imitation — it can represent the caudal fin of a small fish, or the shuck of an emerging adult; and it can be used to add a bit of attraction to an otherwise dull nymph. Well-known examples are the addition of a lime green/phosphor yellow tag to a Stick Fly, or the red tag to a Worm Fly. Alternatively the fluorescence can be added to the thorax, thereby allowing the addition of a more natural tail. Be careful not to overdo the fluorescence — green tags in particular should be kept reasonably short. It seems that whereas fluorescent red tags are effective at any depth, the green/yellow is not so effective very close to the surface; it is therefore worth tying green tag Stick Flies on fairly heavy hooks.

As an alternative, more subdued colouration can be used in larger quantities: golden pheasant tippets provide both colour and contrast without appearing too unnatural; the yellow crest feathers, too, look natural and incorporate a wonderful life-suggesting appearance. In fact, it is hard to see where traditional patterns would be without the golden pheasant: Dunkeld, Mallard and Claret, Connemara Black, Invicta, Teal Blue and Silver, Grouse and Green, Cinnamon and Gold, Woodcock and Yellow, Watson's Fancy, Silver Doctor and many more patterns all point to its proven effectiveness.

THE PERFECT ALL-ROUNDER

If a committee were asked to meet and design an all-round fly which was attractive yet realistic, they might well opt for a silver body. At times these can be devastating, though they can be inconsistent; it is therefore advisable to tone down the effect by making the front half of the body out of a more natural material. Seal's fur would be a good choice, and red is the obvious colour since it attracts trout, represents the gill covers of fish, and is found in some hatching buzzers.

Golden pheasant tippets provide the perfect tail, since they have the contrasting colours orange and black, and could be taken for either a buzzer shuck or a small fish. A hen or soft cock hackle is needed to provide extra movement, and this should contrast with the existing colours. Black is an excellent all-round colour for trout, and can often bring out their aggressive instincts, particularly in brownies. Finally, the large amount of silver on the body requires a wing to complete it, but since the emphasis is slightly more on attraction rather than exact imitation, the best feather would be the black and white teal.

A GOOD EXAMPLE

Techniques for tying flies specifically to catch fish are best exemplified by describing one: the Soldier Palmer for instance is not only a fairly simple pattern to tie, it is also one of the most successful stillwater trout flies ever invented. It has two vital attributes, each of which would be sufficient in its own right. First, it reminds the trout of a whole variety of food items. Adult and hatching buzzers and sedges are perhaps the best known, but there are other species such as shrimps and red ants. Second, since the eyes of most freshwater fish are more sensitive to the red end of the spectrum, it has the unquestioned ability to attract and raise trout, especially supplemented by the water disturbance from the hackles.

Several variations have evolved, but the following dressing is fairly typical:

Hook: Size 10–14	Rib: Gold tinsel
Body: Red wool or seal's fur	Hackle: Palmered red game

This allows for a great deal of interpretation in the dressing, and it is therefore essential that its design is directed towards its ability to catch fish rather than to adorn a fly box. The correct balance between attraction and its natural appearance must always be borne in mind, and this depends strongly on the water conditions as well as the trout's diet. The dressing should incorporate just enough colour and hackle disturbance to attract fish but without overdoing it, so that it is still sufficiently insect-like to be taken with confidence.

It may be argued that the purpose of the Soldier is solely to attract fish to the team, rather than actually taking them, so that they will see the more imitative offerings on the nearby droppers. For example, a buzzer fished below a bushy Soldier can sometimes be a killing tactic, and in these circumstances attraction rather than imitation is the essential purpose of the fly. However, tying a fly which is too unnatural can be unwise, because when a trout becomes wary of a fly he may be put off feeding altogether, irrespective of how natural any other adjacent pattern may appear. Knowing that every fly on the cast is sufficiently natural not to raise any alarm signals can add greatly to confidence while fishing, and although certain tactics may swing the balance more towards attraction rather than imitation, it is still important that the balance is not lost altogether and that it takes due account of the prevailing water conditions.

Several tyings are required to cover all eventualities, and unless care is taken this can easily get out of hand. One basic skill is being able to decide which variations are necessary and which should be ignored. Each fly ought to be tied with a particular purpose in mind, rather than being selected on the basis of its appearance in the vice. Randomly chosen options can lead to a loss of confidence while fishing, and a lot of time wasted in pointlessly changing from one pattern to another.

Hook choice is a fairly straightforward decision: the Soldier is principally a fly for fishing high in the water, and the correct hook is the lightweight Kamasan B400 in a size 10 or 12. It can also be used to great effect on a sinking line, though for this purpose (and in general for flies smaller than size 12) the thicker wire of the Drennan Wet Fly Supreme is recommended.

The body is usually specified as wool or seal's fur, although a whole range of materials including herls and silks can be used. Wools and silks produce very neat bodies which may look attractive in a fly box, but which can appear rather dead in the water. Herls can impart a very enticing movement to a fly, but in this case there is plenty of movement provided by the palmering. Seal's fur has a ragged translucence which suggests life and which perfectly compliments the hackle movement. To achieve the right effect, though, it is important not to tie the body too tightly, and to tease the fibres out a little. Some experts tease out some of the fur to trail behind the fly as a form of tail.

Most fishermen have their favourite shade of red for the Soldier Palmer. Sometimes this is based purely on what they think looks right, which is usually totally unsatisfactory; others have experimented with various different shades and chosen a colour which seems to perform best overall. This tactic is by no means perfect either, since it fails to take account of the need for different colours under different conditions.

Coloured waters often benefit from a large, bright red body because it is easily visible; at Grafham, for example, where the water is often coloured by a preponderance of green algae, scarlet flies can be particularly effective. On clearer waters, far more actual takes — rather than swirls, plucks and follows — often result from a duller fly. A size 12 with a standard red body is a good all-round performer, but with larger flies it can help to darken the shade right down to claret, since the larger the fly, the more likely is the trout to be put off by a garish colour. This is probably why the crimson-bodied size 10 Fancy, which is essentially a Soldier Palmer variant, has proved to be so successful on waters such as Rutland.

Although it is important to obtain the right compromise between attraction and natural appearance, it is sometimes possible to get the best of both worlds. When large red midge occur on the water surface, a hot orange Soldier — often referred to as a (palmered) Grenadier — in a size 10 both attracts the trout and resembles the natural.

On a dull-bodied fly, it would seem that the addition of a bright tail can often add to the attraction without impairing the natural appearance. It is nevertheless important that this is not overdone; the rule is to shorten the tag with increasing brightness. The Fancy with a short reddish-orange tag illustrates this point; it also has a large, soft hackle.

Most people assume that palmered flies should employ cock hackles, and that by far the most appropriate are the very stiff feathers from expensive genetic capes. Nothing, however, could be further from the truth, since stiff hackles lack the all-important quality of movement which plays such a major role in the effectiveness of a trout fly.

Perhaps the best all-round compromise is the soft cock hackle typical of those found on Chinese capes. These have plenty of movement and yet are sufficiently stiff so they do not cling to the body. A good quality hen hackle, however, is acceptable and probably preferable for calm conditions.

As conditions become rougher it is necessary to increase the water disturbance created by the hackles which should stand out against the natural motion of the water; this can be achieved by a stiffer hackle, but in really rough conditions it often pays to add a deer's hair head to the front of the fly. The Soldier Muddler

Success with a sparse, soft palmer in a light ripple

creates a great deal of disturbance, and can also have a soft body hackle to provide some movement.

The number of hackle turns is often omitted but needs to be considered very carefully. In rough water which requires greater disturbance to attract the trout, heavily hackled patterns are much more effective, although they are completely unnatural in calm conditions. So a Soldier for use in a moderate ripple has two turns round the head — these project just beyond the hook point — and three of the same length along the body. In calmer conditions the head hackle can be removed completely, and the effect of the palmer can be reduced by stripping one side off the feather before tying. Rough water often requires some quite drastic measures, such as half a dozen turns round both head and body. Some Scottish and Irish patterns have some quite amazing combinations of hackles, a notable example being the Loch Ordie — and remember the Soldier Muddler!

Fishermen can have great success with brightly coloured hackles, but it is unusual for such patterns to perform consistently. A great advantage of the Soldier is its consistent success based on natural representation. Hackles generally represent wings and legs; a light to medium red game is a safe bet and unlikely to be rejected. The fly can be made to stand out more by adjusting the body colour; playing around with hackle colours as well may simply increase the number of variants to an unmanageable level.

Ribbing holds the palmer in place, suggests segmentation and provides a degree of flash. Thin wire may be perfect on a neat silk body, but does not stand out sufficiently through seal's fur and palmering. On the other hand, a broad tinsel might rob the fly of its natural appearance, and although it might perform well on occasions when the fish were responding to flash, its overall behaviour would be unpredictable. The ideal compromise is therefore to stick to something like a fine gold oval tinsel, though copper or silver may be equally effective. The chosen variations in body colour, size and hackles must be logically based, so you have a good idea of what variant to use on any given day. The use of several different tinsels, however, would add a confusing degree of uncertainty to fly selection.

THE CHOSEN FEW

There are a vast number of flies available and even if you could collect them all, it would be impossible to have sufficient expertise to know exactly which one to use in any given circumstance. Fortunately this is not necessary since very many flies serve an equivalent purpose, and only one is actually needed. For example, it should not be necessary to have both a Silver Invicta and a Silver March Brown, a Bibio and a Zulu, or an Appetiser and a Jack Frost — it only leads to confusion, and it is our firm belief and practice that the contents of the main fly box should be restricted to a couple of dozen patterns.

Imitative flies: (top row, left to right) Perfection Buzzer; Damsel Nymph; Gerald's Midge; (second row) Corixa; Appetiser; Diawl Bach; (third row) Submerged Buzzer; Blagdon Amber Nymph; (bottom row) Pheasant Tail; Green Tag Stick; Stick Fly

Dry flies: (top row, left to right) Hare's Ear Emerger; Squirrel Sedge; Crimson Emerger; (middle row) Shipman's Buzzer; Mole's Hopper; Dry Black; (bottom row) Drone Fly; Red Ant; Dry Grenadier

Suggestive flies: (top row, left to right) Soldier Palmer; The Fancy; V1; (second row) Silver Invicta; Dunkeld; Connemara Black; (third row) Green Panacea; White Sedge; Caretaker; (bottom row) Crimson Bibio; Red Tag Stick; Wingless Wickhams

Pulling flies: (top row, left to right) White Muddler; Bibio; Original V1; (middle row) Cole's Muddler; Vindaloo; The Fancy; (bottom row) Soldier Muddler; Wingless Wickhams; Mad Hatter

It would be unwise, however, to throw away patterns which have succeeded in the past or which could be useful in special circumstances, or which we know are being used successfully by other anglers; after all, traditional patterns have a proven track record over many waters and very many years. Thus we always have one or more boxes in reserve, although we try to select from the main box first as an aid to clear thinking.

The choice of the top flies is obviously subjective — a Bibio is not necessarily better than a Zulu just because that is our particular preference. We may like one fly over another because it was particularly successful on a given day when the alternative was not used. Nevertheless, the two dozen or so flies listed below form a very comprehensive first line of attack.

The patterns are associated with the three categories discussed earlier: imitative, suggestive and pulling flies. A formal concise dressing is not given; we prefer to incorporate this with each description to assist an understanding of the thinking behind the pattern.

Submerged Buzzer (Imitative) Buzzer fishing is normally associated with the surface, but it can be a very effective technique on the sinking line, and a heavyweight buzzer is an ideal choice for the point fly on a floating line. Although many anglers take great delight in trying to imitate buzzers exactly, one of the most simple textbook tyings is extremely effective as a submerged pattern. Black, crimson, claret or green drake seal's fur is dressed fairly sparsely round the bend of a Kamasan B175 size 10 hook and ribbed with fine gold oval tinsel. The thorax may be peacock herl or mole, with white baby wool breathers tied in forwards over the hook eye.

Lightweight Buzzers (Imitative) Buzzers fished high in the water obviously have to be dressed on lightweight hooks, but less obvious is the need to modify the dressing, since a peacock herl thorax seems to be less effective high in the water; thus the different dressing immediately distinguishes between the lightweight and sub-surface buzzer without having to look more carefully at the hook gauge.

There are two different forms of surface buzzer, each very effective but in slightly different circumstances; both are tied on lightweight Kamasan B400 size 12 hooks. Gerald's Midge, tied in crimson, green drake or light olive seal's fur, is slightly more suggestive of a whole range of nymphs and is therefore more general in its appeal. The slim seal's fur body is dressed on the straight shank of the hook only and is ribbed with fine gold wire. This merges into a thorax incorporating a 50/50 mix of orange and brown seal's fur, covered with a wing case of cock pheasant tail fibres. The tail comprises ginger cock fibres and is left fairly long to give the impression of a shuck.

The Perfection is a close imitation of a dark buzzer, and has accounted for many residential trout including a 7¼lb brownie from Chew. It is particularly effective

JD with a 7¹/4lb Chew brownie

during an evening rise. The slim body is dressed slightly round the hook bend using the dark fur from the root of a hare's ear, and this combines with the fine gold oval rib to produce a very realistic body profile in the water. The thorax is a 50/50 mix of mole and black seal's fur, with short white baby wool breathers tied in forwards over the eye of the hook.

Diawl Bach (Imitative) This is a Welsh fly, introduced to the Bristol reservoirs by Stan Pope where it has become an indispensable pattern in most local fly boxes. It is a good representation of a buzzer with shuck attached, although it can represent all sort of food forms. It is best fished as a point fly on a heavy hook and, most importantly, should only be moved very slowly if at all. The tying is simplicity itself: two strands of peacock herl forming a short body on a Kamasan B175 size 10 hook, with a reasonably long tail of light red game cock fibres kept together, and a false beard hackle of the same material swept well back.

Pheasant Tail (Imitative) There are many variations of Pheasant Tail, but this pattern has brought us consistent success on many waters. The body is tied from the lightest available cock pheasant centre tail and ribbed with fine silver wire. It has a long light ginger tail, a peacock herl thorax, and two turns of a Greenwell's hen hackle at the head. Tied on a Drennan Wet Fly Supreme size 10 or 12, it is a marvellous point fly, but will perform well anywhere on the cast. It can often take difficult fish which fail to respond to other patterns.

Dry Buzzer (Imitative) Dry buzzers have only really come into vogue during the last few years, but they are surely here to stay. Even the simplest patterns can be tremendously successful, and the buzzers popularised by Dave Shipman must be the classic example. These are tied on lightweight hooks (the Kamasan B400 size 12 is ideal), and consist solely of seal's fur bodies along the straight hook shank. They are ribbed with fine flat gold tinsel, and have fairly prominent white breather tubes fore and aft. It is tempting to associate the breather tubes with buoyancy, but their main purpose is so the angler can see the fly. To keep the fly afloat, tease out the seal's fur fibres and ensure that they are well 'Ginked' or 'Permafloated' at the bench. Fiery brown is a favourite colour, but black, claret and V1 mix are also successful.

There are numerous variations on the Shipman buzzer: white feather fibres can be used on top of the fly, invisible to the fish but easily seen by the angler, in place of the woollen breather tubes — this makes the fly less specific to buzzers and therefore more generally applicable to a wide range of conditions.

A semi-dry alternative is to use two to three turns of a 'Ginked' hackle around the front of the fly, while leaving the body untreated. The body therefore submerges and the fly becomes an emerger pattern, and there are definitely occasions when these are preferred by the trout. To maintain visibility and buoyancy, it is important to incorporate some (white) elk hair fibres in the top of the hackle.

Corixa (Imitative) This fly should be weighted to achieve the required motion of the natural, and the body built up with white floss silk and a pheasant tail fibre back to match the air bubble. The only viable variation that we know is to incorporate a tinge of yellow in the body floss, since this is a colour frequently found in stillwater naturals. The fine silver wire (or even tinsel) over-rib is an important addition, as are the two paddles which should be represented by goose biots or pheasant centre tail fibres, tied in at the head and swept back at an angle of 45 degrees to the body. Most patterns are tied with a false beard hackle to suggest the legs. The optimum hook is a Drennan Traditional Wet in sizes which range from 10 to 14 to cover the wide variation in the natural.

Langford Damsel Nymph (Imitative) This can be tied weighted or unweighted on a size 10 to 12 Drennan Carbon Nymph hook and is both effective and extremely simple to tie. Three strands of olive-green ostrich herl are used to represent the tail, abdomen and thorax. The abdomen has an over-rib of fine copper wire, and the

Dean Hayes with a 24lb bag from Horseshoe Lake

thorax a wing case of pheasant fibres which are left overhanging the abdomen slightly to represent the wing buds. A dyed olive-green beard hackle of hen or partridge fibres, well splayed out, completes the tying.

Appetiser (Imitative) Although usually classed as a lure, the Appetiser is as imitative as they come, and can be made more so by replacing the normal green and orange hackle and tail by (dyed) bronze mallard. The squirrel tail over-wing contrasts perfectly with the underlying mobile white marabou to suggest a lifelike fry. The white chenille body, usually ribbed with oval silver tinsel, is best tied on a wide gape hook such as a Drennan Traditional Wet size 10.

Green Panacea (Imitative/Suggestive) This little fly will represent green sedge pupae and damsel nymphs. Although damsels appear large, many do not reach maturity since they are taken at a fairly early stage by the trout, and long-shank hooks are therefore not always necessary. The tying is simplicity itself: green olive seal's fur on a size 12 Drennan Wet Fly Supreme, ribbed with fine gold oval tinsel, and finished off with two turns of a soft green olive cock hackle and a tail of the same material. Dean Hayes, MC's ten-year-old nephew, caught the heaviest-ever limit on it from Horseshoe Lake: five fish for 24lb.

Stick Fly (Imitative/Suggestive) This fly is all too often associated solely with caddis larvae, but it can also represent buzzers and many other aquatic items. If it is tied with no tail or with ordinary feather fibres, the same comments apply as for the Diawl Bach. However, it is usually tied with a fluorescent green or red tag, at least on the Bristol reservoirs, and this makes it much more of a suggestive/attractive pattern. The following has caught us very many trout: three strands of peacock herl on a Drennan Wet Fly Supreme size 10, with a small tag of phosphor yellow/lime-green silk wrapped around the hook shank, and 2–3 turns of badger hen hackle.

Blagdon Amber Nymph (Imitative/Suggestive) This is an ideal representation of the amber sedge pupae and is particularly effective in the early morning. It also works as a general pattern, and takes more than its fair share of trout when they are feeding on daphnia. The amber seal's fur is ribbed with fine oval copper tinsel on a size 12 Drennan Wet Fly Supreme, and has three turns of a very mobile brown back partridge hackle in front of a peacock herl thorax.

Squirrel Sedge (Imitative/Suggestive) Long before stillwater dry fly fishing became so popular, this pattern was proving to be generally effective on any water. Tied on a lightweight hook such as a Kamasan B170 size 12, it has a pheasant-tail body, three turns of a light red game hackle and a squirrel-tail wing.

Mole's Hopper (Imitative/Suggestive) The Daddy-Long-Legs seems to work right through the season, irrespective of whether any naturals are present. There are many favourite tyings for this fly, but the Hopper is an adequate imitation and is probably more generally applicable. It should be tied on a slightly heavier hook such as a Kamasan B170 size 10, to help set the fly in the water. The seal's fur body can be anything with a natural appearance, such as olive, ginger or light brown; Mole's Hopper is a mix of 30% ginger, 30% yellow and 40% olive green. The six legs are knotted pheasant tail tied back along the body, and two to five hackle turns are employed depending on the wind strength. In fishing this fly you must have the patience to let it lie static for as long as possible on the water — ignore rising fish and wait for a trout to find it.

Right off the top

Caretaker (Suggestive) This fly suggests a range of emerging nymphs, but has very definite powers of attraction due to the combination of white jungle cock eyes over the thorax, and a large amount of silver in the body which contrasts with the dark fur from the root of a hare's ear. The fur tapers from nothing at the end of the body to a well-teased-out thorax. Flat silver tinsel starts in touching turns around the hook bend, then gradually opens out towards the thorax. Because of its emerger profile, it is tied on a lightweight size 12 Kamasan B400 hook.

White Sedge (Suggestive) The White Sedge fits comfortably into the ubiquitous category; it covers most situations throughout the season, and its general appearance adds to its effectiveness. It is highly visible and yet appears sufficiently realistic to be taken by residents as well as stock-fish, and commands a great deal of respect from those who have had the opportunity to use it. The fluorescent white wool body is tied on a Drennan Wet Fly Supreme size 12 hook and ribbed with fine gold wire. The hen pheasant centre-tail wing contrasts nicely with the white body, and this is reinforced by three turns of a dark red game palmer; two turns of a longer version of the same hackle at the neck add movement. The hot orange feather fibres in the tail add even more to its attraction.

Dunkeld (Suggestive) The Dunkeld in its standard form is tied on a size 10 Drennan Wet Fly Supreme with genuine white jungle cock eyes and no orange palmer; this is perhaps the pattern which approaches most closely a sunk line panacea. It seems to work on all waters, for browns and rainbows, residents and stock-fish, and will take them whether they are feeding on buzzer, daphnia, fry or anything else. We never use the palmered version; its slender, unhackled form seems to be far more suggestive of life — perhaps this is why it is not so killing on the floater. Having said that, the three of us were once sharing a boat on Grafham, and ten rainbows in succession homed in on the Dunkeld, ignoring all six of the other flies which were on offer!

Silver Invicta (Suggestive) The one fly which we cannot really understand but which we would never, ever be without, is the Silver Invicta. We use the normal dressing, which unlike many commercial offerings employs the correct hen pheasant centre-tail wing, on a size 12 Drennan Wet Fly Supreme. It tends to fish best when slightly submerged (an intermediate line is ideal) in bright conditions, but it can vary from being unbelievably killing when the fish will ignore all else, to a complete and utter flop which even the most stupid fish will leave alone. On several occasions we have neglected it following poor performances, then tried it as a last resort, and it has resulted in vital fish being caught during a competition.

It is not always unpredictable: in a size 10 during July it is an extremely consistent fry imitation. This is one of the most exciting times on Chew, when the brownies in particular gorge themselves and 20lb plus limit bags can be the order of the day — if, of course, you have a Silver Invicta!

Connemara Black (Suggestive) The Connemara Black tends to be neglected on many English stillwaters, and its reputation from Ireland and Scotland should be exploited more. Although it can be deadly for rainbows, this is most definitely a fly which will attract brownies: early season on Chew it is a fantastic bob fly which can be held in front of the boat and will bring them up from nowhere. It is also a good sinking line pattern, and in particular we have fond memories of its effectiveness on the Hi-Speed Hi-D at Loch Leven. We cannot improve the standard dressing on a size 12 Drennan Wet Fly Supreme.

Soldier Palmer (Suggestive/Pulling) It has already been shown in great detail (see pages 105–8) how this pattern can be used as a suggester or a puller depending on the method of tying, but two particularly successful variants will be discussed here. The Fancy first had tremendous success in a gale during a Benson and Hedges Regional Final at Rutland. This original pulling version incorporated seven turns of Greenwell's cock hackle round the throat and a further seven down the body. An alternative, more suggestive version has subsequently evolved for less exciting water conditions, employing five hen hackles at the front and three down the

Two more brownies on the Connemara Black

body. In both cases the crimson seal's fur body is tied on a Drennan Wet Fly Supreme 10 and ribbed with fine gold oval tinsel. The tail can be red or orange wool or silk.

The V1 is a splendid example of how our combined thinking has contributed to the invention and development of a trout fly. It was originally the first of a series of experimental variants on Grenadiers (its name is short for Variant One), and is undoubtedly a pulling fly in which two different fluorescent seal's furs, DRF phosphor yellow and DFM red, combine to give a striking effect in the water. It is tied on a size 12 B175 hook, with three turns of a honey cock hackle both round the neck and as a palmer. The tail is of hot orange cock hackles. When adult red midge are present, giving it imitative properties as well, it can be absolutely lethal. Because it is so visible, however, it should be removed from the cast if it fails to bring fairly rapid success.

The striking yet erratic success of the V1 led us to develop a more consistent, suggestive tying which retained some of the pulling qualities but did not raise so many alarm bells. The end result was to change the seal's fur body to a mix of three parts orange, two parts tobacco and one part yellow, to tie it more thinly on a lighter size 12 B170 hook with a softer hen hackle, and to use gold wire in place of the fine oval tinsel. In order to add a little more attraction to what was now a relatively drab fly, a flourescent hot orange woollen tail replaced the feathers.

Bibio (Suggestive/Pulling) The same comments as for the Soldier Palmer apply, *viz* the suggestive and pulling variations. The standard pattern has a black seal's fur body with a red band in the middle, fine silver ribbing and a black palmer and neck hackle, and it is enhanced as a pulling fly if fluorescent red or orange is employed. When used as a suggestive pattern, it is advisable to use a dull red band of seal's fur. Our favourite tying (the Crimson Bibio) has no band at all, replacing the black palmer by a crimson hackle. 'Bibio' refers to the Latin for hawthorn and/or heather fly, and it can be deadly when they are on the water fished either dry, or drowned on an intermediate line. When dark buzzers are hatching it can raise fish very effectively, but the more educated residents tend to reject it at the last minute.

Wingless Wickhams (Suggestive/Pulling) This standard pattern is simplicity itself to tie with a gold mylar body and a darkish (our preference) red game hackle and palmer. It can be tied in various ways depending on its use; on a size 12 Drennan Wet Fly Supreme it is a marvellous general pattern which is worth a try at any time — it can even be effective when the trout are on fry.

Mad Hatter (Pulling) The Viva is all too often associated only with early season or stock-fish, but it is also a killing pattern for residential trout at any time of year. Our variation on the Viva seems to bring out the aggression in trout, and there have been several occasions when it has selectively taken brownies which tend to be territorial and therefore less tolerant of this black and green intruder. We have used the fly to great effect on the educated brownies of Loch Leven, and even on rivers, brownies and rainbows will attack it from nowhere.

We favour the mobility of marabou for the black wing, with a fluorescent green wool body on a Drennan Wet Fly Supreme size 10: simple, but very, very effective.

Vindaloo (Pulling) Ever since Brian Leadbetter wrote about the Peach Doll, there has been so much mystique and baloney associated with getting the right shade of wool that the fundamental reason for the fly's success has been overlooked: its effectiveness is from pure visual attraction, and as such it is best tied with the hottest, most fluorescent and hideously striking orange available. It does not matter whether the body is of wool, chenille or whatever, and although we incorporate an orange marabou wing to add some mobility, it is the bright body which is the key to the fly's success. In coloured water, it may be worth persevering with the fly for some time; in other conditions the fish cannot fail to see it, and if there is no response after a quarter of an hour at the most, it should be removed.

One more for the Mad Hatter at Langford

Muddlers (Pulling) Muddlers are particularly useful for pulling in a big wave where quite a large disturbance is required to attract the trout's attention. There are numerous variations, but we have found that three patterns, tied on a size 10 Kamasan B400 hook, are sufficient for most purposes. First, the Soldier Muddler is simply a Soldier Palmer with a deer hair head in place of the neck hackle (see page 119).

Second, Cole's Muddler can be extremely effective in a wave when the fish are responding to flashy flies such as a Wingless Wickhams. On Chew it once caught us a double limit of residential rainbows in an hour when there was a strong wind blowing into the dam; such conditions are always worth investigating since the currents created by the water pounding a dam wall can bring all sorts of food to the surface. The fly has a gold body with a matching wing and tail of aligned golden pheasant tippets.

Finally, the White Muddler is particularly useful when the trout are tuned into fry. It has no wing or palmer, but the white deer hair fibres in the head are left uncut over the fine white chenille body and marabou tail.

5

COMPETITION FLY FISHING

BACKGROUND

There is no doubt at all that competitions are good for the future of fly fishing. Most readers will know at least something of their history: how the present system has evolved from the early Scottish events into a full-blown international scene, and how sponsorship and big business are now attracting more and more devotees to the fold.

Despite this vast increase in interest the angler, whether organiser or competitor, must keep his eye very firmly fixed on the original objectives of competition, as declared by the governing body of each of the Home Countries: to promote contact, friendship and communication between anglers, through the medium of competitive fishing. The Home International series seeks to do just that, in the form of two meetings each year, held in rotation in England, Scotland, Ireland and Wales. The host nation provides the venue, and teams of fourteen anglers compete using traditional loch-style skills and methods — always from boats. The spirit at such events is superb, and those who have ever represented their country have lasting memories, not just of the fishing, but also of friendships made, stories exchanged and ideas shared.

This is far from the tooth-and-nail fracas that those critical of competitions would have you believe. Competitive fly fishing is about sharing a glass of wine with your boat partner at lunchtime, giving successful flies to unsuccessful opponents and, more specifically, about promoting an acceptable face of angling to the growing anti-bloodsport lobby.

In competition at almost every level, the 'International Rules' are frequently quoted. These are intended to cover every eventuality when fishing traditional loch style 'front of the boat', and when drifting in a reasonable breeze. Drogues are permitted to slow the drift of the boat, but apart from that, success is largely dependent on the skill of the individual competitor; the size of fly is regulated, as is the number of flies on any cast. Simple angling etiquette and good manners, and a respect for the conventions of the boat, are all that is required for a good day out.

In view of the anti-bloodsport lobby, the weigh-in is one area where we should all take great care to be whiter than white. Photographs in the angling press of masses of dead fish do nothing for us or our sport; fish, both alive and dead, should be treated with respect, and whilst no one would detract from the pride of a victorious angler, surely it is better that he is photographed with his best single fish of the day and perhaps a rod, rather than with upwards of twenty dead trout at his feet. Competitive angling is about skill, and photographs like this serve no useful purpose. In some competitions there will inevitably be bumper catches and it is only natural that the fishery concerned should want to publicise the fact that the fishing on their water is capable of producing such results. However, it is in their interests, too, to see that fishing maintains a clean image, and a little restraint in the field of photography is no bad thing for all concerned.

There is a competitive element to most things in life these days. If some fishermen choose to turn this aspect of the sport into a major event — and many

The end of a competition day

thousands enjoy just this — then surely it is not for any other angler to decry their enjoyment; and a strong competitive element may even be good for the long-term future. It is the promotion of traditional values, techniques and ethics, and this alone, which will save angling from the predations of those who would otherwise see it destroyed. Therefore, if it can lead to a shared understanding between fishermen on an international basis, then the contribution to the history of fly fishing will be even greater.

It seems to us that sponsorship should be welcomed to our sport. Benson & Hedges have made a major contribution in developing this aspect and their series is very popular; it is wonderful to experience the atmosphere generated at every stage of the heats. Above all, it is seen as the ideal vehicle to promote the very concept of competition, to introduce competitive fishing to the general public in a palatable, watchable and enjoyable form. And all of us, whether competitors or by-standers, should support such a move.

TACTICS

So much for the theory and philosophy: let us now turn to the tactics, and look at some of the methods and techniques that have made Bristol fishermen so successful in recent years. *All* aspects of the tactics discussed elsewhere in this book are employed in competition fishing: the points that follow here are specifically relevant to competitions. Somebody once said that 'winning isn't everything'. We heartily agree, but just might add 'winning isn't everything, but it beats the hell out of coming second'!

To succeed in to-day's competitive fly fishing, any angler will need to be fully proficient in all the basic skills — the overall standard is extremely high, and there is little or no place for the raw novice; and what follows here must really be considered as 'advanced competition tactics'.

Practice Day Almost all the major competitions are preceded by a practice day, and for the serious angler these are not to be missed. It *is* possible to compete without them, but the added element of confidence they provide is normally indispensable. Even then, practice day is about very much more than just confidence.

Whether it is new to you or well known, you should try to cover the whole water during practice day. You can then sort out the hot-spots, identify areas to be avoided, and work out probable 'first choice' locations for match day. Even if the event is for individuals rather than teams, it is worth agreeing with friends that you will pool information on practice day, as many waters are simply too big or too diverse in character to be fully covered by one angler.

Keep an open mind; also, it is rarely worth taking more than two or three fish from one location — far better then to register the successful flies and move off to another spot. The chances are that no one will have seen your success, and you may have your own private hot-spot on the morrow. Even if everyone does know the location, sitting on the fish all day will only make them nervous and harder to tempt on match day.

Practice day is to build your confidence. Good groundwork, knowing your preferred fishing locations, with confidence in proven fly patterns, and you are already well ahead of the game. You must, however, be flexible: there will be times when conditions change radically overnight, and you must be prepared for a whole new set of circumstances on match day.

Match Day Complete preparation is absolutely vital to a successful day, and this begins at home, in the hotel and in the fishing lodge car park. It will be disastrous to find that you have left a landing net behind, forgotten your Hi-D line, or have no spare spools of monofilament. Once on the water you will not be able to return to the car for coffee flask, rain jacket, scissors or floatant. Most anglers have their

Lighter moments on the Test

own mental checklist — some even write it all down, as the adrenalin that flows in any major competition is very real, and memory lapses can be crucial.

Tie your spare leaders — keep them on empty leader spools — as it is much harder to tie up new leaders on the water, particularly on windy days or if fish are showing all around. Pack your fishing bag in a logical sequence so you have everything instantly to hand. Do *not*, however, take too much kit with you: it will only be a burden, and loose gear around your feet can be a real nuisance. Be thorough, but be rational about what you take on board.

Boat Partners Where possible (in internationals for example), arrange to meet your boat partner on the evening before match day. It is far better to reach mutual agreement over preferred locations, and a pint or two will cement relations and make for a pleasant day.

There is no point in keeping secrets from your boat partner, either, especially in terms of flies being used. *You* may need help from *him*, so at all times be open and honest about flies, line density and methods. If he is being successful watch his technique closely and learn from it. Indeed, you should be watching *all* fellow competitors constantly, as somebody might be having terrific results with an off-beat tactic. Watch, to see whether other anglers are using floating, sinking or Hi-D lines, and check whether anyone has found fish at a feeding depth.

Harmony in your own boat is very important; your boat partner may be from an entirely different walk of life and with a radically different philosophy, but that matters not. Enjoy his company, exchange ideas, and you will have a good day out. You may be paired with someone who talks a bit *too* much, but it is better just to nod politely and give the occasional 'yes' or 'really' — in fact, switch on auto-reply, and just concentrate on your own fishing!

Weather This is a fundamentally important factor (see Change Days, pages 53–5) affecting location and all aspects of technique. You must be able to read the water and translate the previous day's findings into a positive policy for match day. Has the wind changed? Is it much colder/warmer? Will food items be blown to a different location? Is it much brighter/darker, and will this affect the efficiency of your preferred fly patterns? All these things must be assessed before even the first cast is made.

Boatcraft This is a much underrated aspect of competitions. Whilst most boat partners understand the basic pre-requisites, there are still those who will, without warning, do things like tap out their pipes on thwart boards, wear dayglo yellow shirts and rock the boat in a flat calm with about sixteen false casts. All you can do is grin and bear it, and point out (diplomatically of course) the error of such ways — but you also need to make sure that your *own* boatcraft is beyond reproach.

Choosing bow or stern position is the first job of the day. Generally speaking, you can cover fish more easily in the stern, but you will see more in the bows. This has to be viewed against both the weather conditions (the bows are good in a big wind), and the boat handling ability of your partner.

After a lot of angling pressure, fish can become quite boat-shy. In events such as the Benson & Hedges heats, by the third day the fish are likely to be very spooky indeed. Longer lining is an answer here, and so too is choosing bow position in the boat, as you will see the fish more easily and be able to cover them at greater range.

In general though, boatcraft is about being quiet in the boat, handling oars and engine with care, and keeping a low profile. Never cross another boat's line, and always give a wide berth when motoring back up a drift. If you are fishing near to bankside rushes, or down a wall or along an island shore, cut the engine well in advance and either drift to the chosen spot or use the oars — this will cause far less disturbance to the fish.

Tactics Tactics for competition are much the same as those employed in a normal day out. What you *will* need is a higher level of concentration and a more enthusiastic yet flexible approach.

Every day's fishing has a pattern to it. If early morning sees the fish moving on the surface, the choice of floating line is easy. Choosing between intermediate and a slow sinker at lunchtime is harder, as the fish may be holding (and feeding) at four to five feet; equally difficult is locating them at the end of a hard day, when Hi-D lines may be needed. You must be continually flexible in your approach, and be prepared to change lines many times in a day. Remember that fish travel in both directions, up and down — they can start at the surface, be ten feet down at lunchtime, and stay there for the rest of the day. But just as easily they can be back on top at mid-afternoon — the angler needs to be constantly vigilant for all signs of movement.

Many things can fool or frustrate you, and losing fish is perhaps the worst. Apart from using absolutely top quality hooks, there is little you can do to avoid this, other than adopting a philosophical (very) frame of mind! However, there are some circumstances when you will need to modify the strike, particularly when fishing deep with sinking lines, when only a tightening of the line is required. Fish that follow on the surface and take with a real bang do *not* require a hard strike, either — a positive tightening, to 'lift' into the fish, is enough. In both of these cases, an over-zealous strike will either miss the fish or result in a very light lip hooking or broken leader.

It can be particularly hard to bear if you see a fish, cover him perfectly, and yet he fails to respond. If the usual change of fly or retrieve fails to work, a more radical remedy might be needed. It is important to realise the contributory factors here: boat pressure may be making the fish wary, or perhaps they are pre-occupied with a very specific food item which can be identified either by a close look at the water or by using a marrow scoop. 'Pressurised' fish are another matter; the best solution is to move to a quieter part of the lake, or at least to move well away from the crowds. The problem is that it takes a strong effort of willpower to leave moving fish and make such a move.

This principle is at the heart of any change of tactics in competition, whether changing from floating line to sinker, or from wet fly 'pulling' to static dry fly: anglers worry about the time it takes to change, and the possibility of wasted time with the new method. Our answer is: *don't* worry, be flexible, and *do* be prepared to change lines, tactics and location many times in a day's fishing. It is

'Did I qualify?'

fundamentally wrong to stick to the same technique all through the day, as this will not take into account either the weather or the feeding patterns and habits of the fish.

The Percentage Approach There will be times in competition when nothing is showing, very few fish are taking, and both trout and fishery seem to be in a lethargic mood. Three or four fish will represent a very good bag, and these are days when you should adopt the 'percentage approach'. This involves standardising many aspects of your style, and using proven tactics that offer the best percentage chance of success. Use flies that are known to be killing patterns for the water and time of year, and lines to suit water temperature and depth. Use the exploitation process, which means sticking rigidly to floater, intermediate and fast sinker for half an hour each, in the hope of finding the trout's feeding depth.

In all 'percentage' fishing, use the absolute standby fly patterns — proven flies that have shown their value for many years. Unless you find solid evidence to the contrary, perhaps through the marrow scoop, these flies offer the best chance of success.

The Black Box Possessing many hundreds of flies in many different boxes can lead to confusion and match day is no time to be 'spoiled for choice' — you should have a fair idea from practice day on just which patterns you will be using.

We favour the shortlist principle. In our 'match day box' we have a maximum of twenty flies, including those that caught fish on practice day. If one pattern has been particularly effective we may well have half a dozen, on different hook sizes and in different gauge hook wires.

Fishing in Crowds An unfortunate aspect of some competitions is that stock-fish tend to shoal together in particular places, boats follow them, and fishing gets crowded. Regrettably, too, many fisheries insist on a big stocking prior to a match, in the hope that a large catch result will reflect well on them; this can turn what might otherwise have been a good competition into nothing more than a lottery, as many of the real angling skills are negated by too many stockies.

However, there are times when fish do congregate in specific areas and the anglers are obliged to follow them, and there are then some aspects of fishing that are worth remembering. First, use finer leaders: if your fly is swimming in a more lifelike manner than the rest, it is more likely to be taken. Second, give yourself as much room as you can, especially between you and the boat in front — there is rarely an advantage in covering water that has just been drifted by another boat, unless the fish are hard on the bottom.

Netting Always net your own fish, no matter how big or how difficult the conditions. If you let your gillie or boat partner do the job he may easily make a mess of it, which leads to strained relationships, to say the least! Netting is a precise art; only you can really know when your fish is ready for the net, and only you can coordinate net and rod to perfection. In particular, do not show the fish the net any earlier than you have to. Look after your own fish, and keep them wet to conserve weight.

Overall Attitude Your overall frame of mind on match day is almost as important as your angling ability. Too many anglers get so keyed-up that they are on edge all day, unable to relax, and therefore unable to fish properly. A little adrenalin is a good thing as it sharpens the senses, quickens the reactions and helps concentration; but too much is counter-productive: you will strike too hard or too fast, get over-excited and fail to react in a logical manner to your fishing.

The best competition anglers are those who are able to concentrate for long periods of time, and yet can genuinely relax and enjoy the day's fishing. This frame of mind is hard to achieve in a full International, yet will serve you well if you can manage it! Combine it with the conviction that you can win on every day, add to it a general proficiency in all the nuances of technique, and you will be well on the way to your National Final!

6

THE MAJOR
STILLWATERS

The information given so far has been of general application to the majority of stillwaters. Nevertheless, each water has its own peculiarities, and so a brief outline of the four major English reservoirs is in order. The survey has to be selective, but should not be taken as a criticism of other lakes — the choice has simply been restricted to those which are probably most relevant to the largest number of fly fishermen, and the aim is to give the visiting angler sufficient information so he can make a reasonable first attempt at achieving some success.

There is no great amount of detail about the recommended fly patterns, since those described earlier in the book are applicable to all these waters. Rather, the discussion has been limited to the small number of flies which are particularly effective on the water concerned. Obviously, the only way to really know a water is to make several visits, and to tune your own fishing techniques as more knowledge is acquired.

We have a great deal of local knowledge on Chew, but have also fished Bewl, Rutland and Grafham on many occasions. Although we have some very definite ideas on these three, we decided that the descriptions would be put on a firmer basis if we called on the opinion of local experts. Dave Shipman and Brian Leadbetter gave us some valuable information on drifts for Rutland and Grafham respectively, and Jeremy Lucas provided us with an extremely detailed description of Bewl.

By way of general observation, the water clarity is lowest in Grafham, and highest in Rutland and Bewl; Bewl is much narrower than Rutland and to a lesser extent Grafham, with Chew again lying between the two extremes. Chew, however, is at the extreme shallow end of the league, whereas depths at Rutland can exceed 100ft. These factors should all be taken into account when tackling the individual waters.

Contours can have a significant effect, and can be used to locate the whereabouts of trout; and so the very first thing the thinking angler should do before visiting any new water is to find out as much as possible about them. Unfortunately, very little information is given away on such features, and the angler has to rely on general rules without any obvious explanation on where to fish. Contour maps usually

Lake Vrnwy

exist for the major reservoirs, although you may have quite an effort in obtaining a copy; and even we had to admit defeat for Bewl Water. The other three descriptions are, however, accompanied by a contour map which should reveal definite indications — irrespective of any local folklore — as to likely hot-spots.

BEWL WATER (JEREMY LUCAS)

Bewl Water, a multi-fingered reservoir reaching towards the Sussex borders from Kent, is one of the most heavily fished waters in the country, yet it is rarely crowded. Of the 'big four' it is generally the easiest to fish, being 'trickle-stocked' with upwards of 50,000 trout annually in its 770 acres. These are predominantly rainbows, selected and grown-on in the Southern Water Authority's own hatching and cage systems; their policy is also to maintain brown trout stocking at around 10 per cent of the total and there is a small amount of natural breeding by the brown trout.

Most visiting fishermen consider Bewl one of the loveliest man-made fisheries in the country, vying with Chew Valley and Rutland's South Arm for beauty. Because of its complicated shape and careful management it offers fascinating fishing: like all big reservoirs, it can produce days of six fish (the limit) in six casts, and others when the best local anglers struggle to find taking fish; but these extremes are rarer on Bewl than on any other major fishery and it is noted as a very consistent water throughout the seven month season. In non-extreme conditions good fishing style is invariably rewarded.

Bewl has always been a 'headline' water. In 1986 it produced a series of very large, *naturally grown-on* rainbows unprecedented in the history of reservoir fishing — a dozen of these broke the 10lb barrier. I was lucky enough to run into one of these giants while loch-style drifting in Hook Straight with a size 10 Mallard and Claret on the point: she weighed 10lb 2½oz after a ¼lb of snails had been spooned out!

For competitions Bewl is ideal, having more than fifty identical boats available and plenty of space. There are 15 miles of bank, produced by the many folds, arms, points, bays and peninsulas, and more than 10 miles is available for bank fishing. The most noted areas for the bank angler are New Barn, Bramble Point and Seven Pound Creek in Hook Straight; Ferry Point and the Nose in Copens Reach; Rosemary Lane and Goose Creek (early season); Dunsters Bay and the bank between Dunsters and Ferry Point on Bewl Straight. The most consistent drifts are described later (pages 135–9).

Although the usual stillwater fly-life is abundant, Bewl is known for one insect in particular. Where Grafham is acknowledged for its huge buzzers, the 'race-horses', and Chew for the red or 'Grenadier' buzzer, Bewl has the most incredible populations of damselfly. For bank and boat angler alike, to ignore the damsel is to meet distress.

The ubiquitous midge is present in many forms, though few of the very large species show in any numbers. Sedge — grousewings, long-horns, silver-horns, cinnamon and a few great reds — are good in some years (1985/6/7), but surprisingly poor in others (1988). Snail populations were astonishing during 1986, then all but disappeared in the following two seasons. Like the Canadian pondweed which can choke miles of bank, they will return when nutrient and biological features allow. The coarse fish, though held in some degree of check by the SWA, are second only to those in Grafham and Rutland. There are huge roach (I have seen many 2–3 pounders), and in consequence fry can form shoals like wide ribbons, hundreds of yards long. Another consistent food-form over the last five seasons has been the corixa; also various ephemerids, mostly pond olives found at the bottom of Bewl Straight, though these are rarely important.

As a general rule, you are likely to find that at Bewl, a trout will have been feeding on the following, in descending order of incidence: midge (pupae and dry), damsel larvae, corixae and aquatic beetles, fry, daphnia, snail, sedge, alder, olive.

The relevant season would alter some of these in terms of importance.

As general patterns, variants of the Pheasant Tail, Hare's Ear and Midge Pupa are supreme for the more imitative angler. The Bewl Green nymph in its original form as described by Chris Ogborne is an excellent summer general pattern, ideal for the middle dropper position either for the bank nymph angler or the drift fisherman. Over the last two seasons the Bewl Bridge Fly-Fishers Club team has developed this pattern with various materials, including dyed olive hare's mask fur and golden pheasant tippets, sometimes with small white goose biots or jungle cock as cheeks.

Various damsel nymph imitations have come to the fore at Bewl, and none more deadly than that designed by local anglers John White and Robert Barden. Their nymph is simple and sparse, consisting of dark olive seal fur for both abdomen and thorax (well teased out), and ribbed with heavy copper wire; there is no hackle, though there is a tail of dark olive cock hackle-points. This pattern is usually dressed on a Drennan Traditional Wet size 8.

Successful traditional wet flies for Bewl are numerous. Several well-known locals put great faith in the Black Pennell and Black Spider, Mallard and Claret, Silver and Standard Invicta, the many black and green Viva-Montana variants, Grenadier and Soldier Palmer. With Wingless Whickam variants in summer and Stick patterns in spring and summer, most eventualities are covered.

When the trout come heavily on the fry, which most seasons happens some time in August and builds up right to the end of October, the floating fry patterns are deadly. Peter Firth's deer hair version is the simplest and possibly the best. Tied with white deer hair and trimmed to a torpedo shape, with a sparse tuft of white tail, this pattern is greased and fished without a retrieve. White marabou and Appetiser-type mini-lures also take their toll of fry-feeders, though rarely with anything like the success of the floating fry. To date there has been surprisingly little experimentation at Bewl with mink and rabbit fur fry imitations as there has at Rutland and Grafham.

Spring Drifts Extreme localisation of the trout is the main problem presented by spring conditions. There is a lot of deep water, even close to many banks, and this tends to be relatively unproductive. In most springs, the beautiful Hook Straight does not produce anything like the quantity of trout as does Bewl Straight; it remains a 'specimen-hunter's' area, where you are not likely to find large shoals of stockies.

For many seasons the winds throughout most of April have been hard northerlies and north-easterlies, and drifting off the north shore, as far west as Seven Pound Creek Point and most especially in the region of Bramble Point and the cages (between Bramble and Bryants), has proved very consistent. So too has drifting from Dunsters Point, past Goose Creek, then down towards and into Tinkers Marsh (very temperamental) and Rosemary Lane.

Bewl Water

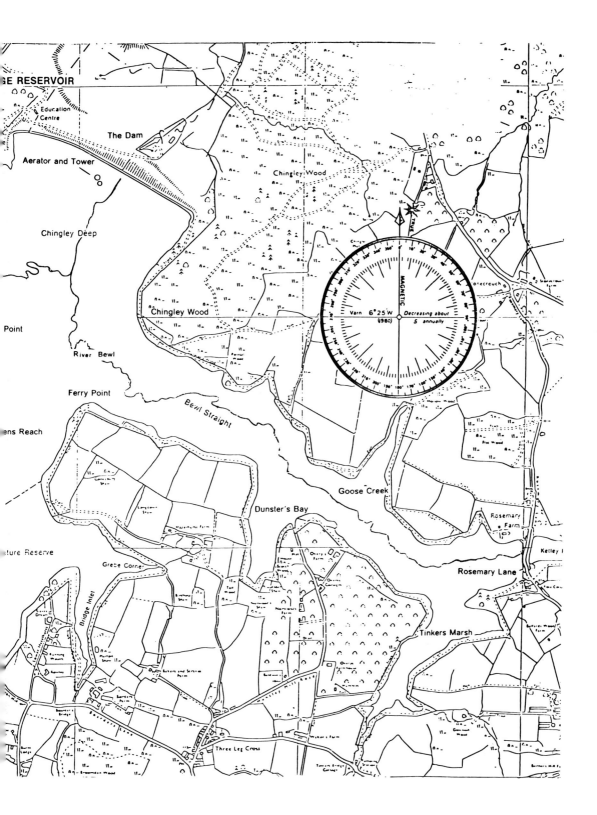

The experienced drift fishermen try to keep within sixty yards of the bank. The central 'Bowl' area does not often produce well at this time of the year, though drifts around Chingley Point can be productive, especially if the wind is blowing onto the point. When the wind shifts to the west and south-west, there are some exceptional areas. Goose Creek, half-way down Bewl Straight, tends to hold huge shoals of rainbows — sport is furious when the wind is blowing into the Creek. However, when the wind is blowing across its mouth or, worse, out of the Creek, then the shoals tend to migrate very quickly across the reservoir to Dunsters Bay or even farther east to Rosemary. So if Goose fishes badly, try Dunsters, and vice-versa; the trout might be in very small areas of these big bays. These areas have distinct locations which tend to collect huge numbers of stockies at this time of year; later in the season they become big fish lies.

Ferry Point delineates Bewl Straight from Copens Reach, and is outstanding throughout the year. Drifting as close to the bank as possible here — either from the Straight, the Bowl or the Reach, depending on wind direction — will nearly always produce fish.

If wind allows, a drift along either shore of Copens can be good (or totally hopeless) in spring — if one shore does not produce any action, the other often does. The Nose itself is very consistent, and for drift fishermen is best when the wind is out of the north-east, driving you right down into this bay's throat. Bank fishermen allowing, boat anglers like to get in very close to the bottom of this bay when the wind is from the south-west, so that they are blown gently out along the western shore of Copens, often all the way up to Beauman's Point. It produces gorgeous, quiet nymph-fishing on the drift.

Summer Drifts The fish are much more spread out, and drifts are usually far longer, often not necessarily close to the banks. There are good, deep-water buzzer hatches and trout are caught on the surface right over the deepest parts of the Bowl, upper Bewl Straight and Copens. Even so, drift fishermen often find the most consistent results near the various banks. Strangely, the eastern end of Bewl Straight usually dies as if a switch had been thrown — the coarse fish, including huge pike, are most numerous down here. Copens Reach invariably comes into top form and virtually any wind direction produces good drifts. Hook Straight usually develops into the most popular area some time in late May, all the way beyond New Barn and Pine Bay to Brown's Inlet, Whyligh and Three Creeks. The prevailing westerlies and south-westerlies are ideal, allowing long drifts past the many features of this area. Boat fishermen often begin right up in the little stream beds that enter the lake here, drifting out over the very shallow water. It is as close to paradise as you can get in reservoir fishing.

A hard easterly is very bad at Bewl. We are not far from England's east coast, and sometimes in May and June we get strong, cold easterlies off the continent which produce some of the most difficult drift and bank fishing. The soft, warm easterlies of high summer are quite different, and yield some of the best dry-fly fishing on the drift. In a cold easterly we head for the sheltered upwind shores and fish deep, as slowly as possible, under drogue — though it is often worth trying the bottom of the Nose, Brown's Inlet and across Bramble Point. As soon as the east wind diminishes and it becomes warmer, we search for the buzzers and damsels which inevitably appear.

High summer is best handled with long drifting, Grafham-style. While spring causes extreme localisation, the problem in high summer is the opposite — the drift fisherman finds a small shoal but loses them quickly, perhaps finding another in a few hundred yards. These rainbow shoals move quickly, and anchoring boat anglers find they are on fish for half an hour and then lose them for several hours unless they move along the bank. The most consistent high-summer areas are the corners of the dam, the long drifts over the Bowl in a westerly or southerly, or the more intimate areas of Hook Straight and Copens. One of the most popular drifts on Bewl in summer is in a southerly from Ferry Point, across to Chingley Point and onward to the dam. In a northerly, the drift is reversed.

Autumn Drifts Without a doubt drift fishermen do best very close to the bank during autumn, because the corixa and fry are there and are usually the dominant food-forms for the trout. In better sedge years, hatches may hold the fish out over slightly deeper water, though the shallows will give the best results. When there are dense mats and fringes of pondweed and ranunculus along the shores, the best fishing of all comes right at the edge of the weed, or in holes and channels through it. Short zig-zagging drifts are best, which blow the boat onto the weed or shore; then pull back out a hundred yards and drift in again. The south shore of Bewl Straight, either shore of Copens and most parts of Hook Straight offer tremendous short drifts. Fish are caught almost right up on the bank in inches of water, especially in tumbling waves. They are nearly always on corixa or fry, or occasionally snail.

Special Areas Particular features which at times become dominant are the cages and the aerator. Trout tend to congregate in the cage area for the free meal of pellets which sink through the mesh — there are sometimes hundreds of very large fish here, approaching the 10lb class, especially when there are neither huge shoals of fry, nor populations of snail, to draw these giants out into the main body of the lake. There is a hundred yard limit around the cages where fishing is not allowed, though these large trout are occasionally taken by lure and nymph fishermen anchored in this area. This is not the only place where big fish are caught — we have taken fish in the 4–10lb class as far from the cages as Three Creeks, Tinkers Marsh and Copens Reach. They are always drawn to the best food source for the season.

The oxygenation and cool water effects produced by the aerator, locally called 'the bubble', also draws fish at times of high temperature and/or calm weather. The shoals of stockies here can be unbelievable, but it is just a pity that so many anglers tend to collect here to rake through this easy prey. In early 1987, during warm weather, Peter Firth and I took one drift over the bubble with traditional wet fly teams. We each hooked three trout straightaway, and the sight of six fish simultaneously thrashing on the surface made sure that we did not go near the place for the rest of the season: fishing that is too easy is not fishing at all.

In major competitions the bubble is turned off and the stockies are usually caught then within a quarter of a mile, still in tight shoals and usually close to the dam, in the yacht bay or off Chingley Wood.

CHEW VALLEY LAKE

Chew is inevitably our favourite water because it represents home ground to us, but even if it were hundreds of miles away we would undoubtedly make the journey time and again. It is one of the finest stillwaters in the British Isles, set in the beautiful Mendip countryside, and where the angler can expect superlative top-of-the-water sport at virtually any time of year.

Chris Klee with a magnificent 4lb residential rainbow taken from Chew Valley Lake

Chew's success lies in its basic anatomy. The average depth of water is only 14 feet, and there are vast areas of shallow water with hugely prolific fly life. There is immense variety in the shoreline — dense areas of rushes mingle with withy copses, long points link in with green and intimate bays, tree-lined banks are interspersed with open lawns: the whole angling environment approaches perfection.

The bank fishing is good, but it is for the quality of its boat fishing that Chew is justifiably famous. There are almost too many drifts for us to single out any particular favourites, and like most waters, different parts of the lake fish especially well at different times of year. The following are classics:

NORTH WIND: North shore to Denny Island
Over the False Island
Over Nunnery Point

WEST WIND: Villice Bay
Into Wick Green
Across Roman Shallows

SOUTH WIND: Off Moreton Bank
Across Roman Shallows
Into the dam

EAST WIND: Out of Herriotts
Into the dam
Across False Island

Generally it pays to seek out the shallower areas, unless there are obvious concentrations of fish holding the deepwater banks. When the 'Grenadier' midges are showing, which can be anything from late May onwards, you can expect a lot of surface activity from the fish which can and do become totally preoccupied with this food form; at such times the cast can include both Grenadiers and Soldier Palmers, fished right on the top. Indeed, so useful is the Soldier Palmer on Chew that it would be a very brave angler that left this fly off his cast!

Artificial flies for Chew are fairly predictable, and a shortlist is easy: Green Tag Stick Fly, Claret Buzzer, Connemara Black, Dunkeld, Soldier Palmer, Grenadier, Pheasant Tail, Viva, Wingless Wickhams and Mallard and Claret. In addition, the Ombudsman and Persuader are good in early season. The Silver Invicta comes into its own when the fry are showing, and on any bright day. In late season, Appetiser and Corixa can have their place and dries like the Hopper or floating buzzer can also work well.

Bank fishing needs a lot of thought on Chew, and the successful anglers will seek out the quieter corners, exploring the margins with weighted nymphs. In general terms, a slower retrieve with floating or intermediate lines will work far better

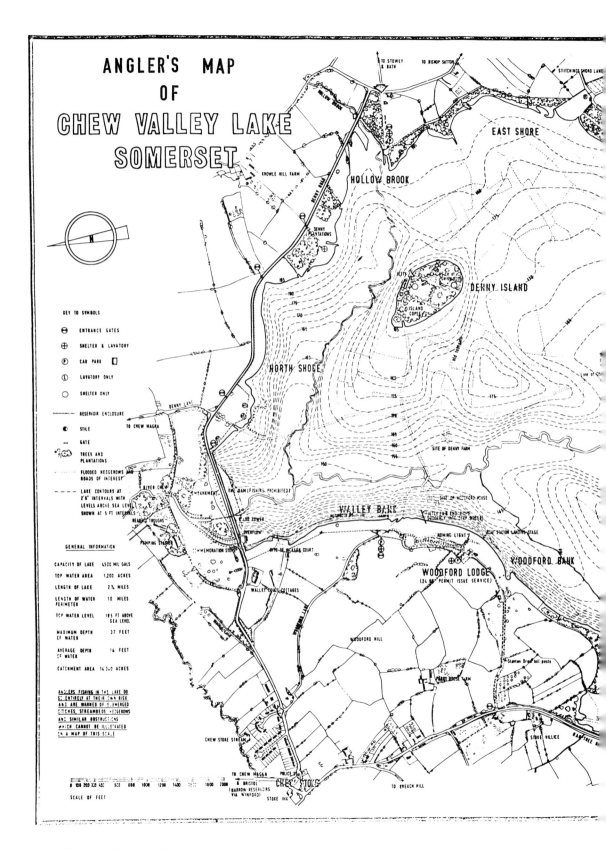

(depths quoted as feet above sea level)

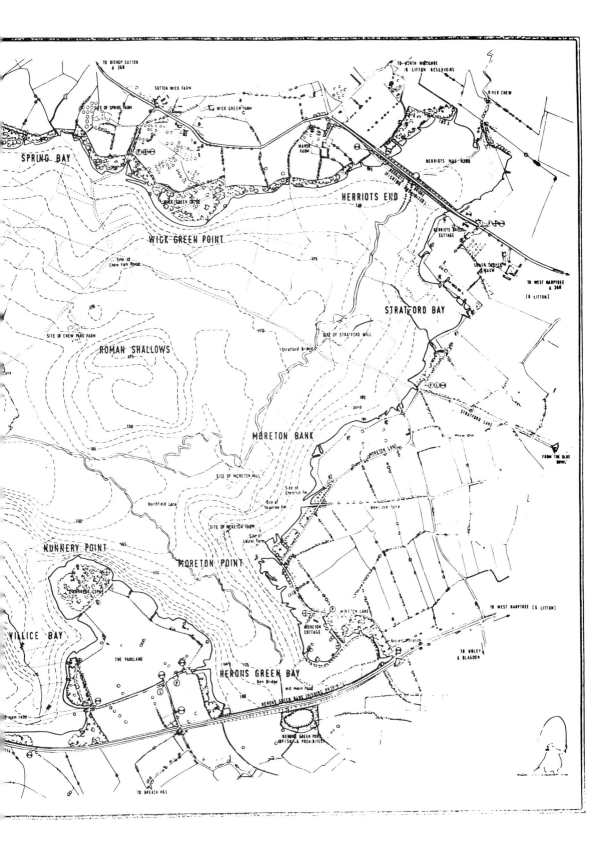

SPRING BAY

TO BISHOP SUTTON
A 368

SUTTON WICK FARM

SITE OF SPRING FARM

WICK GREEN FARM

MANOR FARM

TO NORTH WIDCOMBE
& LITTON RESERVOIRS

RIVER CHEW

HERRIOTS MILL A368

WICK GREEN POINT

WICK GREEN COTTE

HERRIOTS END

HERRIOTS BRIDGE COTTAGE

Site of
Chew Park House

SITE OF CHEW PARK FARM

ROMAN SHALLOWS

LOWER STRODE FARM

TO WEST HARPTREE
A 368
(& LITTON)

STRATFORD BAY

SITE OF STRATFORD MILL

Stratford Bridge

STRATFORD LANE

FROM THE BLUE BOWL

pond

Lane

MORETON BANK

MORETON LANE

SITE OF MORETON MILL

Northfield Lane

Site of Chestnut Fm

Site of
Templeton Fm

NUNNERY POINT

SITE OF MORETON FARM

Site of
Laurel Farm

TO WEST HARPTREE (& LITTON)

NUNNERY COPSE

MORETON POINT

MORETON LANE

VILLICE BAY

THE PARKLAND

MORETON COTTAGE

Ancient monolith

TO UBLEY
& BLAGDON

HERONS GREEN BAY

Ben Bridge

old main road

HERONS GREEN BANK (FISHING PERMIT)

HERONS GREEN POOL
(FISHING PROHIBITED)

TO BREACH HILL

'Not another 4-pounder!'

than faster, sunk-line lure tactics. In late season, and particularly when the weed has died back, the muddy banks of Wick Green, Moreton and Stratford offer real chances of a big brownie, and in such conditions the Worm Fly is a proven favourite. For most of the year though, it is the general suggestive and imitative patterns that really do the damage.

By far the best advice to anyone coming to Chew is to enquire at the Lodge as to where and how the fish are being caught. Bristol Waterworks staff are the best informed of any we have ever met, and are normally happy to share the information. It is a very real bonus that most of the rangers are also fishermen!

The quality of both fish and fishing at Chew is without peer. Much of our philosophy originated here, even if it was honed and modified by experiences elsewhere, and we consider ourselves very fortunate to have such quality on our doorstep.

GRAFHAM WATER

Grafham appears a rather featureless reservoir, without any islands and with only a limited number of bays and promontories. It is also somewhat exposed, and in particular can suffer from cold east winds.

Like most stillwaters, however, there are plenty of areas where underwater contours provide fairly consistent sport. The best all-round spot from the bank is probably the dam which, unlike many other reservoirs, is accessible to fishermen. The very steep contours provide the necessary depth and weed growth for holding large concentrations of trout well within casting range, in spite of angling pressure. Indeed, a problem with bank fishing here can be interference from the boats which also try to make the most of this productive area when conditions elsewhere are hard. Other good areas from the bank can be Hedge End, Savages Point and opposite G-Buoy (where stocking takes place).

The boat fisherman should, of course, exploit the contours — particular areas which are worth exploring, whatever the wind direction, are the false islands at Lymage Shoal (close to H-Buoy) and Sanctuary Bank (close to S-Buoy), and of course, the end of the contours off the stocking area close to G-Buoy. There is always a good head of fish around the Aerator Tower to the north of the lake.

There are many effective drifts, but the following are generally recognised:

NORTH WIND:	North Shallows to Sanctuary Bank
	Church Hill Cove to Butcher's Point
	Chalk Bank to Gaynes Point
NORTH-WEST WIND:	Littless Bank to Perry Head
	Hedge End to G-Buoy
	Savages Point to Lymage Shoal
NORTH-EAST WIND:	D-Buoy to Gaynes Cove
	Pylon to Fishing Lodge
	Harts Bluff to Nature Reserve Hide
WEST WIND:	Rose Garden to Perry Head
	Nature Reserve Hide to C-Buoy
	Savages Point to Hedge End
SOUTH WIND:	Fishing Lodge to Lymage Shoal
	Lymage Shoal to Sanctuary Bank
	Perry Head to Harts Bluff
SOUTH-WEST WIND:	Valley Creek to Hedge End
	Gaynes Point to D-Buoy
	Gaynes Cove to Valve Tower

SOUTH-EAST WIND: South End to East Perry Buoy
                                 Pylon to Hedge End
                                 Hedge End to North Shallows

EAST WIND: Hedge End to Swannery Point
                                 A-Buoy to Gaynes Point
                                 C-Buoy to Nature Reserve

Grafham has three vital characteristics which are often overlooked: first, the green colouration given by the algae, which can sometimes be so thick that it is washed up on the dam wall in the form of a thick soup. This often demands extra colouration, brightness, or water disturbing properties in the fly dressings. Thus a dull red should perhaps be replaced with scarlet or even fluorescent material — in fact, it was on Grafham that the original tying of the V1, with its mix of phosphor yellow and DFM seal's fur, first proved itself as a killing fly during a hatch of red midge, and since then it has continued to be a consistent 'puller'. Flies can also be tied with slightly more hackle than normal.

The second feature of fishing Grafham is that it usually pays to fish slowly, and to allow the trout to turn on the fly before striking. Fishing slowly is generally the most effective technique on any stillwater, but at Grafham it is just that little bit more important.

Finally, the fish at Grafham always seem to be looking to the surface for their food, more so than in any other major English reservoir. Very often there is nothing showing, then out of nowhere takes will come to dry flies and nymphs fished high in the water. Obviously in early season, fast sinking lines have their place, but as the season progresses you will not go far wrong by restricting all your fishing to the floater. Grafham is the one stillwater where we would hardly ever consider using the intermediate, and it is small wonder that so much of the recent popularity in dry fly fishing originated on this lake.

The exception to this floating line rule is when the trout are on daphnia. The massive daphnia blooms of the past have come and gone, but daphnia can produce some fantastic growth rates in the trout. Many lure-fishing patterns and techniques were pioneered in the early days of Grafham, when the daphnia were particularly numerous.

One of the favourite fly patterns throughout the season is a size 12 Pheasant Tail nymph, tied with a green or orange thorax. In April and May black flies can be very effective, and a Black Buzzer fished on a sinking line can produce good bags when nothing is showing. For the main part of the season Soldier Palmers, Silver Invictas, Wickhams and Dunkelds should always be given a fair try, as well as more imitative patterns to represent buzzer and sedge pupae. Towards the back-end both Daddy Long-Legs and fry patterns (such as the Appetiser) really come into their own.

MC with a good Grafham rainbow

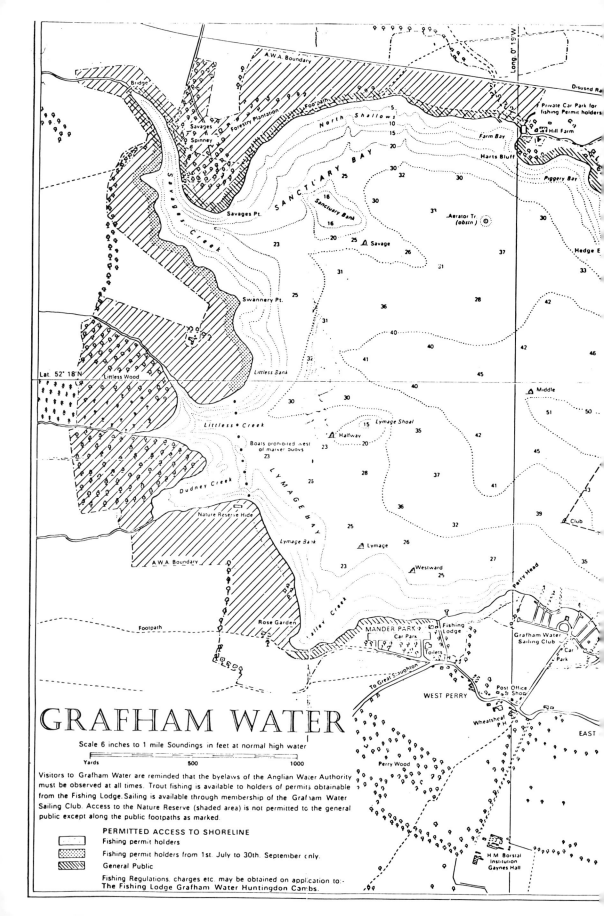

GRAFHAM WATER

Scale 6 inches to 1 mile Soundings in feet at normal high water

Yards   500   1000

Visitors to Grafham Water are reminded that the byelaws of the Anglian Water Authority must be observed at all times. Trout fishing is available to holders of permits obtainable from the Fishing Lodge. Sailing is available through membership of the Grafham Water Sailing Club. Access to the Nature Reserve (shaded area) is not permitted to the general public except along the public footpaths as marked.

PERMITTED ACCESS TO SHORELINE

Fishing permit holders

Fishing permit holders from 1st. July to 30th. September only.

General Public

Fishing Regulations. charges etc. may be obtained on application to:-
The Fishing Lodge Grafham Water Huntingdon Cambs.

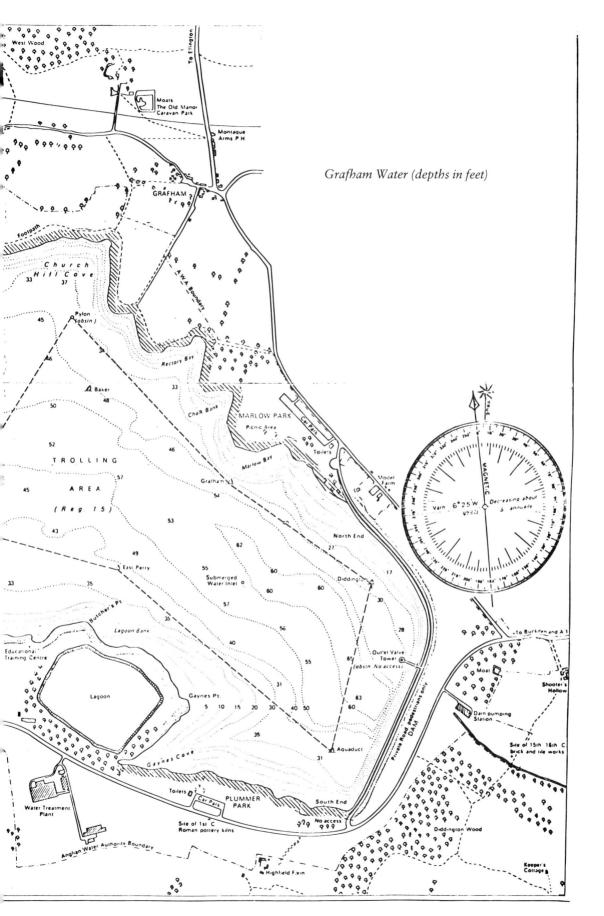

Grafham Water (depths in feet)

RUTLAND WATER

If there has to be an ultimate challenge in fly fishing, then Rutland must be a strong contender. At well over three thousand acres it is twice the size of Grafham, and reservoirs like Chew could be fitted into its South Arm. A very real problem is being spoiled for choice, since to motor from the top of one arm to the other can take a full hour, which is a lot of wasted fishing time.

The many bays and creeks are surrounded by large areas of deep water and become rather like small fisheries in their own right. The action can therefore become very local indeed, and never more so than following a local injection of stock-fish. This first-hand knowledge is a great asset, and on this water perhaps more than any other it pays to cultivate the goodwill of the fishery staff who are invariably well informed.

However, perhaps the most important aspect of Rutland is not its overall size but its great depth over much of its area. Thermoclines develop quickly and persist, and all through the season water temperature can be a vital factor in the way it fishes. A study of the contour map is therefore very important, but it takes many years before even a local angler will really get to know the topography of the place.

A perfect ripple off Normanton

Rutland Water proprietor, Roger Thom

Stock-fish shoal fairly predictably at Rutland, and bank fishing at either end of the dam, Normanton, Sykes Lane and Barnsdale can be very good indeed. In these areas the fish often follow the daphnia, so very careful attention should be paid to the wind direction. The long stretch of bank on the Hambleton Peninsular between Armley Wood and the Transformer is worth a walk, casting every ten yards to try and find the fish.

In summer the water quality is usually superb with luxurious weed beds providing cover. There is a good head of resident and semi-resident fish which offer a challenge to any angler, and prospecting among the weed beds in the secluded reaches of the South Arm with a single nymph or dry fly can be fly fishing at its best.

The best way to tackle Rutland, however, must be by boat. The clarity of the water, the profusion of fly life and the almost limitless permutations of drift make the place a loch-style paradise — any list only scratches the surface of the drifts truly available.

The lake is best classified in three parts: the North and South Arms and the main body, and there is enough fishing in any of these areas to keep most anglers fully occupied for a day, the main factor determining choice of location being the weather. On a lake this size even a moderate wind will push up a big wave, to the extent that a force 6 can make conditions decidedly dangerous.

Fish will change their feeding depth frequently at Rutland, more so than on many other waters. Great flexibility is therefore needed, in changing line densities to find the fish — it is not unusual to have to change from a floater, through intermediates and faster sinkers down to a Hi-D, and then back again, all in the space of a couple of hours. This can be due to movements of food sources, or boat pressure in the relatively clear water.

Rutland Water (depths in metres)

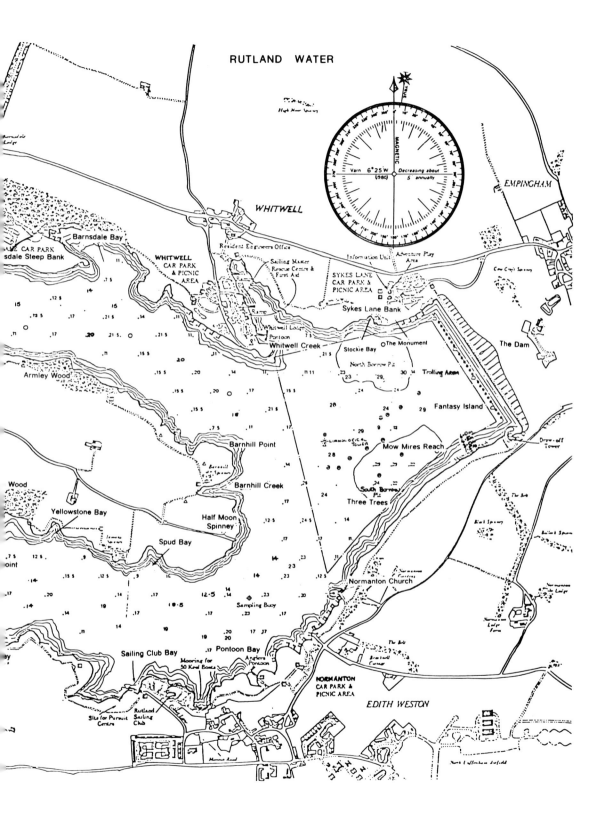

Happy days on Rutland

Open water drifts are good in the main body of the lake, particularly if the aerators are working or when there are wind lanes to follow; drifts in the Arms tend to be closer to the banks or to underwater features. The size of the place means that bank anglers are seldom a problem, and it is possible to drift down long stretches of bank without disturbing anyone, keeping only ten yards from the shore.

Because of the large areas of deep water, Rutland takes a long time to warm up in the spring and the water can be very cold even in May. Fly life therefore takes some time to get going and the staple diet in early season is daphnia; so wind changes are particularly important at this time of year in locating the fish. Fly life in spring is most prolific in the shallower reaches of the Arms, and it can be well worth the long journey to find some moving fish and a good hatch of midge.

Dry fly tactics are particularly good at taking some of the large resident trout — the water is so clear that fish which are cruising at depths of six feet or more can see the flies on the surface; it is therefore particularly important to use double strength nylon.

Rutland is superb in so many ways. The facilities are excellent, the boats are well maintained, and there is always an element of unpredictability about the day. The sport at Rutland is difficult to match anywhere in the country, and its reputation as one of England's premier fisheries is well deserved.

Flies Through the Season

APRIL: Viva (and black flies in general), Stick fly and Pheasant Tail (green tag or thorax), Butcher, Black Buzzer

MAY/JUNE: Shipman Brown Buzzer, Silver Invicta, Wingless Wickhams, Olive Quill, Gold Ribbed Hare's Ear, Grenadier

JULY/AUG: Silver Invicta, Invicta, Soldier Palmer, Drone Fly, general dries (brown green, orange), Silver Thorax, Pheasant Tail

SEPT/OCT: Daddy, Soldier Palmer, Appetiser, Viva, White Muddler, Silver Invicta, Brown Buzzer

Drifts

NORTH WIND: Into Armley Wood from 150yd out
                  Into Sailing Club Bay
                  Out of Old Hall Bay

NORTH-WEST WIND: Across Barnsdale Point (Lodge side)
                  Into south corner of dam
                  Out from Bunds

NORTH-EAST WIND: Out of Dickenson's Bay
                  Along Sykes Lane, 75yd out
                  Into Normanton Church Bays

WEST WIND: Out of Lax Hill
                  Across Dickenson's Bay
                  On to the Boils

SOUTH WIND: Into Barnsdale Creek
                  Out of Sailing Club Bay
                  Into Sykes Lane

SOUTH-WEST WIND: Out from Manton Bank bird hides
                  Across Berrybutts Point
                  Out from shallows by Tim Appleton's old road

SOUTH-EAST WIND: Along Green Bank
                  Into mouth of Hideaway Bay
                  Across Brown's Island

EAST WIND: Out from Green Bank
                  Along Normanton Bank, 60yd out
                  Along Barnsdale high bank

7

IN OUR OWN EXPERIENCE

CO's TALE – A DAY FOR CHARITY

If winter fishing is to be enjoyable, let alone successful, then you have to be very selective in your choice of venue. No matter how attractive the scenery is, or how pleasant the weather, if the fishing is not managed properly then the day out is destined for failure.

It is therefore fortunate for anglers in the Wiltshire region that the Langford Fishery is very well managed indeed. Located in the beautiful Wylye valley between Warminster and Salisbury, Langford is arguably one of the best small stillwaters in the south of England. Run by Paul Knight, whose enthusiasm and energy is immediately evident to the visitor, it is easily identified as being run *by* anglers, *for* anglers. When weather conditions permit, it can produce buzzer hatches to match Blagdon or Chew, and there is always the chance of a fish on weighted nymphs, even on a dour day.

On 4 March 1989 we were expecting the latter. In conjunction with the West Wilts FF, Paul had organised a pro/celebrity match to raise funds for a local hospital. This early in the season he was taking a real chance on the weather — we could very easily have found ourselves facing sleet showers, and ice in the margins. In the event, the exact opposite happened, and we gathered in the car park to the tune of chattering birds, high gentle cloud, and a spring-like day that could have passed as May. In view of our main purpose, which was to raise money for charity, it really did seem as though fortune was smiling on the righteous!

We were representing the Bristol Reservoirs FF, with our friend John Horsey making up the fourth team member. Langford was no stranger to us; we had all enjoyed some very pleasant winter fishing here quite recently, testing both leader rig theories and new deep water nymph patterns. In this respect the place is ideal, as there is a good mix of shallow and deep areas, allowing all line densities to be used during any day out, with a whole cross-section of tactics.

This particular day looked just right. A reasonably gentle westerly was blowing across the main lake into the corner by the Lodge. Calm conditions thus prevailed on the far bank, and until the morning chill had lifted this also provided some

Winning team at Langford

degree of shelter; not surprisingly, this area quickly became crowded. For a while, the fishing almost took second place as we greeted old friends from all over the country who had come to take part. As this was the first major event of the season there were many 'over-wintering' stories to be told and, as ever, anglers like to catch up on the gossip.

However, with so many big competition names present, the sport quickly took over, and we were down to business. John Pawson, fresh from his recent victory in the World Fly Fishing Championships, was quickly in action and so was Brian Leadbetter from the same team. As a 'semi-local' side we felt that some honour was at stake here, and most of us had fish on the bank in the first half-hour. It soon became obvious that whilst Paul Knight had added a fairly generous stocking for the event, there were also some semi-resident fish being taken. This encouraged a switch to more imitative fishing, as opposed to the more basic early season flies such as the Viva and Persuader that we had been using as first line of attack.

It was very much a day for the intermediate line. Virtually no fish were being taken on the floater, and equally, the fast sinking lines seemed to be taking the flies too deep; and the fish were obviously wanting the flies at a very slow retrieve. That the intermediate was ideal was particularly true in the afternoon session, when a slow fly proved, yet again, that it has a year-round versatility.

Far from being put down by the large number of anglers, it seemed that, if anything, the fish were becoming more active as the day progressed. This must have been due in part to the continuing improvement in the weather: the cloud had broken during the afternoon into long sunny spells, and the chill element had completely disappeared. Most anglers were taking advantage of the 'move-on' rule: once three fish were taken in any one place, you changed your spot. We were therefore enjoying all the corners of the fishery, including the narrow neck of the small lake, which was undoubtedly a holding area — the wind was pushing a high concentration of daphnia into this neck, and the fish were feeding hard.

Perhaps the best thing was that almost everyone was catching fish, as well as enjoying the good company. Paul and his staff were continually dispensing a mixture of coffee, good humour and hot soup, all of which were welcome. The good smells wafting from the 'hospitality tent' indicated that something more substantial was being prepared, and when at last the final whistle blew we all headed back to the weigh-in with some enthusiasm.

The best part of 'the result' was that we had raised over £2000 for the charity, a credible performance for only forty anglers. Modesty should prohibit us from saying that we *won* — but it won't! We beat our friends and rivals in Blagdon Fly Fishers by some 8lb, with MC and JD coming first and third respectively. The Trout Fisherman Magazine team came in third, thanks to a sterling performance by Peter Cockwill, just ahead of the very strong Midlands contingent.

The usual post-mortem took place in a very convivial atmosphere, in a lovely warm evening that would have done credit to mid-June — there were even a few fish head-and-tailing out on the lake. It had been a friendly affair throughout, and a wonderful way to set the scene for a new competition year. The quality of the fishing, coupled with the chalk valley location, had many a visiting angler promising himself a return visit to Steeple Langford.

THREE DAYS ON GRAFHAM

The Benson and Hedges Championship has brought more excitement to fly fishing, and done more to promote traditional styles, than perhaps any other single factor. Like most teams, although we go out and try as hard as possible to win, we have tremendous fun and learn a great deal in the process.

The 1986 final at Grafham was no exception. On the practice day, the Bristol Reservoirs team had been split up to cover the whole lake, and our assignment in the morning was to cover the area round the Valve Tower and Savages Creek. It is extremely difficult for three to fish simultaneously, so we adopted our usual arrangement of taking a rest after every fish.

Under such conditions the fishing partner is always tempted not to try too hard to actually land his fish — whereas the third person wants his turn, and is ready and waiting with the net to help boat it as quickly as possible. A simple way to prolong a fight is to show the net to the fish before it is ready, since an apparently beaten fish will gain a new lease of life and go on another run as soon as he senses it. In fact the most efficient way of netting is to scoop the fish out with the net when his head has been lifted just above the water surface. Like this, he does not have the power to turn away, and gets very little chance to see the net.

On this occasion, however, the third person did hold one ace up his sleeve. CO had brought some particularly fine vintage Rioja onto the boat, and had made the rule that there would be no drinking while fishing. Thus there was a fair balance between wanting to fish and selflessly offering to take a little time off.

The temperature had fallen considerably overnight, resulting in very little activity, and with the wine uncorked, we were all volunteering to take a rest. Then at about midday, we started picking up fish on the point to that old standby, the Pheasant Tail. Success on the point fly sometimes indicates the beginnings of a rise, and although in this case it was not particularly spectacular, it was sufficient to keep the interest going. It was during the early stages of this rise that MC caught a fish on a Dunkeld. CO and JD then took trout on the same fly, and the next fifteen minutes saw a frantic change of positions within the boat as fish after fish was landed. A short fishing bonanza is not uncommon on any water, but it is a complete mystery why ten fish in a row homed in on the Dunkeld, in spite of two other perfectly respectable imitative patterns being on all three leaders. The weather was fairly bright, but if Dunkelds always had the same effect on the floater under such conditions, there would be no need to look to any other fly.

As the rise progressed the fish became much more difficult to catch on any fly. This is fairly typical of any rise, when the fish are quite willing to take a wide variety of offerings as they first come up to explore, but soon become pre-occupied as they settle into an established feeding pattern.

A change of tactics was called for; we managed to catch the occasional fish on a dry fly and — perhaps inspired by the generous quantities of Rioja — on some standard lightweight buzzer patterns which we 'Permafloated' on the spot. This was before Shipman Buzzers really came into vogue — and to this day we cannot understand how or why we failed to pursue this particular matter further, ahead of the field.

At the end of the day we had a fairly good idea of the way to approach the match day; we also had some valuable information from John Braithwaite who, being wise to the coloured water at Grafham, had found that the trout were responding well to scarlet buzzers.

Conditions on the match day were fairly similar, though there was a little more wind and some cloud cover. Scarlet buzzers worked extremely well, as did the trusty Pheasant Tail. MC was successful on his Permafloated buzzers, and Steve Pope did particularly well with a lightweight, sparse Soldier Palmer. Throughout the day we could not help noticing how many fish seemed to be caught immediately after cutting the engine, and we did not hesitate to change drifts as often as possible. But the Dunkeld, the star of the previous day, caught very little, and simply emphasised the unpredictability of flashy flies.

At the end of the first day we were just behind our close rivals, the Chew Grenadiers. They had found a shoal of fish on the practice day that no other team had noticed, and true to their name and spurred on by a great performance by Leigh Sennington, had used Grenadiers to great effect.

There was everything to fish for on the final day which turned out to be bright and calm. Fish were not so easy to come by, and even now we cannot understand how the Chew Grenadiers continued to catch on the same methods as the previous day. Most of our team caught steadily on sparse patterns, but it was a late burst on one particular fly which gave us the narrow margin to take first place: until then we had neglected the Silver Invicta, but in the last hour of the competition it selectively took fish which hit it with all the force they could muster.

The perfect day was completed, of course, by the usual excellent ceremony laid on by Benson and Hedges. It was the climax to three exciting days in which we had not only achieved victory, but in which we had learned a great deal. We learned about the use of bright flies on Grafham, about the effect which an engine can have on pulling fish to the boat, about floating buzzers and about the consistency of general imitative flies. Most of all, though, we learned that we can neither explain the inconsistencies, nor ignore the existence, of flashy flies like the Dunkeld and Silver Invicta.

MC's TALE — THE FIRST TROUT

Wentwood Reservoir enjoys a special kind of tranquil beauty which helps one forget all the trials and tribulations of everyday life, so when the Water Authority decided to lease the fishing, it was not surprising that a group of far-sighted local fishermen formed the Wentwood Fly Fishing Association. Most significantly, they quickly transformed a dour water into a first-class fishery, largely due to the amount of unpaid effort put in by the committee — a warning to any prospective lessees.

My very first trout-fishing experience took place here, on a day which, although a little overcast, still seemed pleasant to the uninitiated. My casting skills were virtually non-existent, and it was well worth the extra charge to hire the boat since the only chance of reaching the fish was to get right over them. The rod, reel and line together had cost the princely sum of £18, and a 'fully comprehensive' selection of half-a-dozen flies was neatly arranged on a presentation card.

I shall never forget the problems which beset me. As soon as the boat was in position, the heavens opened and the wind reached storm force, and rolling waves

Edward D. catches his first Wentwood trout

pushed the boat towards the dam wall. After frantically rowing towards the bank, I eventually managed to beach the boat and make for home, wet, cold and exhausted.

It was a sign that fly fishing was well and truly in my blood that, after a quick change of clothes and a few words of encouragement from my dear lady, I was ready to resume battle with the elements. Fortunately, the wind had dropped completely and after eagerly baling out the boat and rowing a hundred yards off-shore, it was time for another assault on the Wentwood trout.

The rather arbitrarily chosen fly seemed to make quite a plonk as it hit the water, sinking quickly and gently pulling the leader through the surface. After a few feet had disappeared, the nylon suddenly stopped dead. This could not be the bottom in such a depth of water, and with the optimistic thought that it might just be a fish, I struck into my very first trout. The surprise could be felt all the way down the line as the trout went on a twenty-yard run with the reel screaming. After cautiously retrieving some of the line, the silver flash of his body could be seen some twenty feet down in the gin-clear water. After two more heart-stopping runs, he was boated and quickly despatched.

For the next quarter of an hour I kept looking at 'my' fish in total disbelief; but within the next couple of hours four more were boated just like him (the limit was six in those days). In every case the line was not retrieved at all; there was really no alternative with such short-distance casting, and no point in doing so since the fish were taking so consistently 'on the drop'. Ironically, a more proficient caster would probably have been unsuccessful since he may have automatically retrieved the fly.

On returning to the lodge, a small group of fishermen were eager to know what fly had done the damage. It is strange how the immediate question always seems to be about the fly, rather than the depth or method of retrieve. They seemed quite indignant when they were told I didn't know, but it was soon identified as a leaded shrimp.

After such an introduction to trout fishing I could not fail to be well and truly hooked, and there have been many enjoyable days at Wentwood since then from both the boat and bank. But there is a moral to this story. The novice who concentrates on the only tactic he knows is unlikely to be confused by a whole selection of techniques, and sometimes he can out-fish even the experts.

JD's TALE — THE ART OF COMPROMISE

One of the most important words in anybody's fly fishing vocabulary should be 'compromise'. So often too much attention is paid to having exactly the right tackle for certain conditions, or to having a precise imitation of the natural during a rise. In fact, a little bit of thought and understanding is usually more important, because trout tend to be far less concerned with fine detail as long as the overall approach is sound.

This lesson was brought very firmly home many years ago and, ironically, it all started with a mistake. Nowadays no-one would dream of going fishing anywhere at any time of year without a dry fly box, but on one of my first visits to Lower Moor this is exactly what happened. Arriving at the fishery on a hot afternoon in early June, there were entries in the book to show that the mayfly season was in full swing. I had never experienced mayfly fishing before, but with the usual confidence that often goes hand-in-hand with inexperience, it seemed a certainty that nymphs like the good old Stick Fly would take their share of fish.

Most of the recognised hot-spots were taken on that Sunday afternoon, and in particular the point on the main lake was fully occupied due to a very localised rise. Whilst wondering how to find a suitable space in the crowd, a mayfly settled on the water in front of me. They are such beautiful insects that I sat down to observe it, forgetting my urge to fish for a while — until it suddenly disappeared amidst the rings of a rising trout. The breeze was blowing the mayfly from the bankside vegetation out into the lake towards the point, but anywhere along this path was a prime feeding area for the waiting trout; the only advantage of being actually on the point was that the ripple had a chance to build up, and helped disguise the angler's presence.

The sudden feeling of excitement that there were fish within reach was followed by despair at not bringing any dry flies. Also, not having had much previous success with dry flies, there was a strong temptation to fish a team of nymphs. Fortunately reason prevailed, because not only were the trout so clearly taking the adults, but nearly everyone else was fishing wet flies and catching very little. Furthermore, in this secluded and windless corner, it was important not to disturb the water, and the constant casting and retrieving of a nymph might have had the opposite effect.

With no dry flies let alone a mayfly, I reflected on whether any wet pattern might have the correct general colour and profile. If so, it might just have a chance of success if only it could be stopped from sinking. Perhaps a wet fly cast very carefully might just stay on the calm surface film, even without floatant which had also been left behind. In such circumstances, it was actually an advantage being away from the ripple on the point.

The mayfly at Lower Moor are the very dark species, classified rather unfairly as *Ephemera Vulgata*. Looking through my box, the nearest representation (to use the word in its loosest sense) was a rather bushy Mallard and Claret. It was cast very carefully to make it alight as gently as possible on the water. It stayed there perfectly, and I remained motionless, sitting down out of the trout's window. After a few minutes doubts were beginning to arise, but at least it was a very relaxing way to fish. And then, without warning, the classic nebbing rise occurred, and a perfect 2lb residential rainbow was hooked in the scissors. There have been few fish which have given me so much pleasure or made such a lasting impression in my memory.

While drying out the only Mallard and Claret in the hot sun, the same tactic was repeated with a Black Pennel; half a minute later a second fish rose, but was missed by striking too soon. On every cast a fish rose, and in less than half an hour on these two wet flies and some still unidentified palmered pattern, I had caught a magnificent limit.

Thus began my awakening to dry fly fishing, and needless to say several more trips were made during this period to Lower Moor with purpose-tied mayflies. On some occasions the fishing was equally spectacular, giving the opportunity to experiment with timing the strike; a delay of about a second was optimum. At other times the trout were much more wary, but then was even more to be learned: the importance of submerging the leader and the trick of twitching a dry fly immediately after it had been rejected — another form of FTA.

Mayfly can, in fact, be a bit of a mixed blessing, for after a feast the trout can 'sulk' for a few days and not be interested in any offering at all. Nevertheless, the advantages far outweigh the problems, and there can be few more exciting ways of learning the art of dry fly techniques.

The laid-back approach

EPILOGUE

This book constitutes the very latest thinking of three totally committed trout fly fishermen. We have included everything in our repertoire and have disclosed ideas and theories that have been consistently proven over the last five years. In a sense we have laid bare our entire philosophy so as to help the reader to be more successful with trout fishing.

Fortunately there are some things in fishing that defy the medium of print. No writer has yet been able to define the pleasures of the English countryside to the degree that it deserves, nor can anyone ably describe the ultimate pleasure of rod and line. There will always be that one extra factor in any fishing situation. Success will depend not simply on the angler's ability and aptitude, but also, and perhaps more importantly, on the 'feel' that he has for the sport. No-one can ever teach this final factor; it comes with experience, it can be acquired over a number of years, but it cannot be taught. It is, however, a most important aspect of our fishing: we are committed to this English country sport to an almost fanatical degree and share a love for the countryside to an extent where this has become an integral factor in our game.

Fly fishing is an evolutionary sport. Just as new flies are invented every year, so too are new tactics. This may involve a simple and minor variation on a theme or it may be a fundamentally new idea designed for a specific angling circumstance. Hopefully we have encouraged every angler to think in this vein, because the most unique pleasure of all is not to be found in learning from others but in the discovery of such new ideas for yourself. We hope that what we have done is to have laid the foundations for such discovery.

INDEX

DAVID & CHARLES' FIELDSPORTS AND FISHING TITLES

The Angling Times Book of Coarse Fishing · Allan Haines and Mac Campbell
Catching Big Tench · Len Arbery
The Complete Book of Float Fishing · Allan Haines
The Countrysportsman's Record Book & Journal · John Humphreys
The Great Hunts · Alastair Jackson
The Great Salmon Beats · Crawford Little
The Great Shoots · Brian P. Martin
Hunting · R. W. F. Poole
Jemima Parry-Jones' Falconry & Conservation · Jemima Parry-Jones
Purdey's: The Guns and the Family · Richard Beaumont
Shooting Pigeons · John Humphreys
Sporting Birds of the British Isles · Brian P. Martin
Success with Salmon · Crawford Little
Tales of the Old Gamekeepers · Brian P. Martin
Training Spaniels · Joe Irving
What Every Gun Should Know · J. C. Jeremy Hobson